The Great Reconstruction

Exactly a century ago, the Westhoek - as the former front zone in Flanders is called - rose like a phoenix from its ashes. The First World War had wiped dozens of towns and villages along the old battlefront clean off the map. After the Armistice in November 1918, the entire Westhoek region was a wasteland of desolation. The plain of the River Yser was flooded; the landscape had been devastated beyond recognition; and the ground was polluted with metals and toxic chemicals. Recovery seemed out of the question. Where on earth to begin? Yet slowly but surely, the Westhoek clawed its way back to its feet. Within a decade, the reconstruction was largely completed.

Resilience and solidarity

The reconstruction stands as a symbol for the resilience of the local population. The first refugees returned even before the war had ended. While they awaited the rebuilding of their homes, they helped with the recovery of the region. There was work to be done! At the same time, social life in the region also began to flourish once more. As early as 1919, local fairs and processions were again taking place, just as they had before the war. Taverns like *'In Tnieuw Bixschote'* offered people relaxation after their long days working in what was known as 'the devastated region'. The religious community also began to re-establish itself.

Tavern 'In Tnieuw Bixschote'
Westhoek Verbeeldt

The level of solidarity shown to the region was great. The Belgian State promised that it would pay compensation for all the damage caused by the war. To make this financially possible, Germany would be forced to pay reparations. Many donations were also received from allied and neutral countries – The Netherlands, Great Britain and even New Zealand – which helped to heal the wounds of war. These donations were mostly in kind: seed, livestock and poultry that would make it possible for the people to feed themselves. Other countries offered cheap loans to fund the reconstruction.

One Westhoek, many stories

Every town and village has its own reconstruction story. In Ypres (Ieper), the *In Flanders Fields Museum* tells how the martyred city and its surrounding region were rebuilt. The *Yper Museum* focuses on the processes of social-cultural reconstruction. Diksmuide also concentrates on the material and social reconstruction of the town. Nieuwpoort devotes attention to the traditional architecture of Jos Viérin, while in Zonnebeke the remarkable oeuvre of Huib Hoste is central. The link between the reconstruction and tourism is explored in Heuvelland, with Poperinge preferring to make children and the sick the main protagonists in its reconstruction story. Langemark-Poelkapelle, Houthulst, Koekelare, Veurne, Mesen, Lo-Reninge and the ***Commonwealth War Graves Commission*** also have their tales to tell, which show how the reconstruction and its con-

Wrecked tanks are a major attraction for the first tourists. This wreck is on the Menin Road, not far from Hooge.
In Flanders Fields Museum, Antony d'Ypres

Ypres, 24 April 1920. The weekly Saturday market takes place among the ruins of the Cloth Hall.
In Flanders Fields Museum, Antony d'Ypres

Church of Sint-Niklaas in Messines
Jan Dhondt

sequences still resonate today. The fact that the landscape of the Westhoek today has a strong homogenous feel owes much to the 'picturesque' architectural style that was adopted, in an attempt to eradicate all traces of the war. In just a few years time, complete villages and towns were rebuilt to their pre-war pattern and the Westhoek was restored to its former glory. Various walking, cycling and motoring routes now take you to the main sites connected with this reconstruction.

Contents

- Ypres (Ieper): the reconstruction after the First World War 7
- Diksmuide rises from its ashes 25
- Nieuwpoort: Follow the Feniks 39
- Zonnebeke: Huib Hoste introduces modernism in the Westhoek 51
- Heuvelland: The Feniks in Heuvelland 63
- Poperinge:
  - Feniks: children of the reconstruction 73
  - De Lovie: Health care after the First World War 81
- Langemark-Poelkapelle: The Poelkapelle tank and other stories 85

- **Houthulst:** From devastated wasteland to proud and independent municipality 93
- **Koekelare** and the link with France 101
- **Veurne**, the 'open' city 105
- **Mesen:** A small town with a great history 111
- **Lo-Reninge:** The Feniks in Lo-Reninge 117
- **From Recovery to Remembrance:** The Commonwealth War Graves Commission (CWGC) in Flanders after the First World War 121

YPRES

Vleteren
Langemark-
Poelkapelle
Ieper
Zonnebeke
Heuvelland
Mesen
IN FLANDERS FIELDS MUSEUM

The reconstruction after the First World War

At the end of 1918, the medieval city of Ypres (Ieper) was in ruin. The Cloth Hall, Europe's largest Gothic building with a civil function, had also been completely destroyed. The reconstruction was long and difficult, but by 1967 the building had at long last been restored to its former glory! Together with St. Martin's Church, it once again represented the face of the city – as it still does today.

Old and new stones

The Cloth Hall stands as a symbol for the resilience of the city and its surrounding region. When you take a close look at the building, you will see that the outer walls contain a mixture of old and new stones. The few pieces of wall that had survived the First World War formed the foundations for the new building. These original stones are darker in colour and some still bear the visible scars of war.

Rijselstraat, 15 September 1919. After the First World War, very little of Ypres remained.
In Flanders Fields Museum, Antony d'Ypres

The reconstruction: a story of many

Different people had different visions about the reconstruction. *The exhibition Feniks: the reconstruction after the First World War* allows you to look over the shoulders of the local people, local policy makers, architects, tourists, artists and many others as they approached the immense challenge of rebuilding Belgium. From April 1919 onwards, the Ypres brothers Maurice and Robert Antony took thousands of photos of the reconstruction of their native region. Their eye-witness accounts offer us a unique view of the resurrection that took place here.

Between hope and despair

The duped population hoped to pick up the threads of their normal lives as quickly as possible. The government encouraged this hope, by promising full compensation for all war damage. This, they said, would be financed by German reparations, which were fixed by the Allies during peace negotiations in Paris. In practice, however, payment of the compensation was slow, as was the provision of emergency housing that had also been promised. This often led to street protests. People lived lives of poverty in temporary barrack villages. Food and drinkable water were scarce. Basic provisions, such as health care and public transport, were non-existent.

'This is Holy Ground' was the message that could be read immediately after the war on placards erected on the ruins of the Cloth Hall.
In Flanders Fields Museum, Antony d'Ypres

Ploughing on...

Apart from the financial support provided by the government, the post-war recovery was primarily undertaken by the people themselves and, in particular, the many people who worked on the land. After the first clearance of the old battlegrounds, the farmers immediately began to clean up their fields and make them fit for cultivation. They rejected tentative plans to plant up the most devastated areas with woodland. With very few exceptions, the old front line area was transformed relatively quickly back into a productive landscape. The newly reconstructed farms had a traditional appearance, but a more rational approach to the practicalities of farming. Out in the fields, everything remained the same: land boundaries were not redrawn. Even so, the disappearance of the typical pre-1914 hedges, which once separated fields and meadows, meant that the Flemish farming environment was transformed from a closed into an open landscape.

Hands off! Holy ground.

If Winston Churchill, who was then the British Minister of War, had had his way, Ypres would have remained in ruins forever. In his opinion, 'A more sacred place for the British race does not exist in the world'. In July 1919, it was decided to leave the Cloth Hall and St. Martin's Church in their ruined state. Huge boards were erected on the rubble, saying that this was 'holy ground' and that not a single stone should be removed. But the British wish to preserve Ypres as a single great monument to the war and as a symbol of the Allied victory never came to fruition. It was agreed, however, that a memorial could be built at the Menin Gate to commemorate the thousands of missing soldiers from the Empire.

How pre-war art was saved

Fortunately, many of Ypres' precious works of art escaped destruction during the war. This art was salvaged from the city early in the conflict by architect/photographer Eugène Dhuicque, acting on behalf of the government. Many private citizens also took precious items with them when they left the city. An exhibition opened in Paris in May 1915 at which all the artefacts on display had been rescued from the Belgian front, with the profit used to assist mutilated Belgian soldiers. Some of these works of art can now be seen in the new exhibition in the Yper Museum.

Front tourism

Although travel to and within the war-torn region was difficult, the first tourists from home and abroad soon began to descend on the old battlefields, using various guides that were published from 1919 onwards. These earliest visitors had a certain morbid fascination with the countless ruined towns and deserted villages, not least because it allowed them to see the places – Passchendaele, Ypres, Messines – where their family and friends had fought or died. People who visited the 'devastated regions' described them as a desert, a desolate and depopulated wasteland. Some, such as the Bruges biologist, Jean Massart, even saw the devastation as an

The American engineer Knox developed a huge machine to level shell-torn ground, but in practice it did not work.
Archives of the Royal Palace, Brussels

ideal biotope for the development of new species of plants. Like many others, he thought it was a good idea to preserve part of the old ruined war zone.

City architect Jules Coomans

The way Ypres looks today was largely the work of one man: Jules Coomans. As the official city architect, he was responsible for the reconstruction of the most important municipal buildings, such as the Cloth Hall and St. Martin's Church. On the Colaertplein, he designed his own home as part of one of the few magnificent sections of facades that had survived the war. Coomans was in favour of a historicising reconstruction, with the pre-war city as its model, and this in contrast to his former colleagues, Eugène Dhuicque and Huib Hoste, who argued for a more progressive approach.

The reconstruction through the eyes of the artists

Many artists came to give their impressions of the devastated regions. One of them was the Canadian artist Mary Riter Hamilton. She was commissioned by the *Amputation Club of British Columbia* to paint the ravaged landscape of Northern France. In 1919 and 1920 she extended her travels in the direction of Ypres and Diksmuide. Her paintings focused primarily on the pioneers who were trying to rebuild their communities among the ruins.

After the war, the government issued premium bonds to finance the reconstruction.
Lottery Museum, Brussels

(Inter)national solidarity

After the war, a renewed form of patriotism stimulated national solidarity. There was a belief that citizens who had sacrificed everything for their country must be compensated for their loss by that country. However, when it became clear that the German reparations would be insufficient to finance the post-war recovery, the Belgian government was forced to introduce a system of premium loans. These government bonds made it possible to rebuild private property with public resources. At the same time, there were also displays of international solidarity. Friendly nations such as Great Britain, Canada and New Zealand, as well as countries that had remained neutral during the war, also offered help, both in kind and in the form of cheap loans. This made it possible for the Belgian people to once again look to the future.

Public and private reconstruction

During the reconstruction period, the repair of public and private property was strictly separated. As a result, the pace for re-building homes and

Identical or 'to the pre-war model'?

The number of buildings that were identically rebuilt was actually very small. This was because in most cases the original design plans were no longer available after the war. Where they did still exist, as was the case with the Cloth Hall and St. Martin's Church, often a number of (invisible) changes were made; for example, the use of concrete for the interior structures. As a result, most buildings were reconstructed to 'the pre-war model'.

Filling the shellholes, Mary Riter Hamilton.
Library and Archives Canada

Advertising for the Vermeulen brewery, with the ruins of the Ypres belfry in the background.
Ypres Museum Collection

housing was much faster than the pace for re-constructing buildings with a public function, like churches and the Cloth Hall. The owners had two options. They could wait to receive their war compensation and then rebuild their houses themselves. Or they could make use of the state system for reconstruction. This was a kind of 'key-in-the door' mechanism, whereby the owner relinquished their right to compensation in return for a new home built by the authorities. This system made use of architects who were not always needed for the alternative of 'do-it-yourself' construction.

The first urban development legislation

Under the influence of the British 'garden city' movement, in 1915 the Belgian government introduced for the first time an obligation to draw up a land usage plan to improve spatial development in the war-damaged towns and villages. However, the practicalities of the reconstruction period put a brake on the high expectations for a more modern Belgium: there were very few far-reaching changes in urban planning in the years immediately after the war.

The first tourist guides for the front region appeared as early as 1919.

British influence

The continued British presence in Ypres during and after the war had an influence on local eating and drinking habits. When English tourists arrived in Ypres, they were pleased to find many of their home 'favourites' in local inns and taverns, including stout. Following the British tradition, many local breweries also made their own Christmas ales, a tradition that has continued to the present day.

A market is held among the ruins of the Cloth Hall in Ypres.
IFFM, Antony d'Ypres

'Architect in Residence' 2020 – Philippe Viérin

In 2012, *noAarchitecten* transformed the Cloth Hall to house the new *In Flanders Fields Museum*, complete with research centre, museum café and tourist office. Through their study of and work in this historic building, they were able to experience and understand why reconstruction was the best option after the First World War. Within the framework of the Feniks project, the IFFM is inviting Philippe Viérin of *noAarchitecten* to reflect on the 'Great Reconstruction' in the Westhoek. What makes this so special is the fact that Philippe is the great-grandson of Jos Viérin, one of the most important reconstruction architects. In addition, Philippe Viérin has also been involved in other

The reconstruction is not yet complete

Even today, more than a century after the end of the First World War, the statues that once graced the niches in the facade of the Cloth Hall remain lost without trace. However, other heritage items, taken by soldiers as souvenirs during the war, continue to turn up all over the world.

Did you know that the repairs carried out to the ramparts in Ypres in the 1990s were still paid for with reparations from the First World War?

L'Emprunt de la Paix: (Peace Loan): In the foreground, a mother is caring for her two children; in the background workers are repairing the damage caused by the war.
In Flanders Fields Museum

renovation and renewal projects, such as the town hall in Lo-Reninge and the Tempeliershoeve (Templars' Farm) in Westvleteren. In other words, material enough for an exhibition and a publication that combine a personal and critical look at the past with a current vision on the architecture and landscape of the Westhoek.

Picking up the threads

Socio-cultural life in the devastated region slowly picks up, thanks largely to the efforts of the people themselves. It is they who transform houses into homes and turn a ruined municipality into a thriving community, all with the same tireless energy and determination.

Back 'home' in Ypres

Architect Jules Coomans and burgomaster René Colaert are strongly in favour of a faithful reconstruction of the city. But reconstructing a city is more than simply building new houses. The people also need to feel at home in their surroundings. The exhibition in the Yper Museum explores the less well-known but more human side of the reconstruction, with a focus on the renewal of the city's socio-cultural life.

Ypres reborn

The people who return need food and accommodation. But they also need a social life. As a result, they quickly restart old clubs and societies, like the various archery guilds. The St. Sebastian Guild in Ypres first reconvened on 27 November 1922. The guild's medieval origins provide a symbolically important sense of continuity.

New clubs and societies are also formed. Not only veterans associations, but also brass

Medard Duchatelez

On 19 March 1921, King Albert visited 'het Groot Kameroen' in Oostkerke (near Diksmuide), the farm of the gentleman farmer and burgomaster, Medard Duchatelez. Duchatelez had earned this honour thanks to the leading role he had played in helping to get agriculture in the region back on its feet. As a director of the Belgian Boerenbond (Farmers' Union) and vice-chairman of the Agricultural Association for the Devastated Regions of West Flanders, he was instrumental in the reclamation of farming land and the recovery of the livestock herd. He also helped to organise agricultural competitions at various places between 1919 and 1922, including Bruges Diksmuide and Ypres. These attracted huge entries, not least because the winners received generous cash prizes.

Banner of the St. Sebastian's Guild in Ypres.
Yper Museum Collection

bands, theatre groups and other social groups of various kinds all appear in 1919 and 1920. 1919 also sees the resumption of cycle racing in Ypres during the St. Peter's Fair. The first 'Our Lady of Ypres' day is celebrated the following year, with the Cats Festival resuming in 1921. People come together to make music, act in plays or even just to drink a good glass of English stout.

More Chinese than Belgians

In the first half 1919, the number of labourers working in the Westhoek for the *Chinese Labour Corps* was estimated at 12,000, far exceeding the number of local residents who had already returned home.

Wooden huts, a temporary church and the first rebuilt houses: Dikkebus, October 1921.
In Flanders Fields Museum Collection

Interior of emergency accommodation in Boezinge.
In Flanders Fields Museum

The story of Leonie Verduyn

The first funeral ceremony in post-war Boezinge was actually a memorial service. Leonie Verduyn, wife of Kamiel Vandenberghe, died and was buried in 1915, but the fighting made it impossible to hold a church service. This was now performed on 26 November 1919 in a temporary barrack church by Pastor Vanneste, one of the great pioneers of the reconstruction in Boezinge. The walls of the chapel were covered in black mourning sheets and there was even a choir in attendance.

Interior of the temporary church in Boezinge.
In Flanders Fields Museum Collection

Business as usual?

Children need to go back to school. There are new births, new confirmations and new marriages to celebrate. The first schools and churches are in temporary wooden structures, but as the 1920s progress, more stone buildings reappear. By 1927, the Meat Hall is ready and offers a home for the Municipal Museum.

Things do not always go as smoothly as planned. In 1930, a crate with weapons donated by the Japanese government to the Municipal Museum arrives in error at the War Museum. The curator of the former sends a letter to the curator of the latter, asking for the crate to be delivered to its rightful destination. As both museums are housed in the same building, this is not a problem: the war museum curator just carries it up the stairs!

A magnet for the construction industry.

During the 1920s, hundreds of architects and building contractors and thousands of building workers came to the Westhoek. Some stayed, but most went home again once the reconstruction was nearly completed.

In Flanders Fields Museum

The In Flanders Fields Museum is every visitor's portal to the history of the First World War in Flanders. It tells the story of life and death in the Westhoek region during the terrible years between 1914 and 1918. The museum explains how and why over a century ago hundreds of thousands of people from all over the world were all part of the same tragic event.

Yper Museum

Here you relive ten centuries of Ypres and the Westhoek, a story of trial and error. On an interactive and distinctive route you discover the medieval city in all its glory. An unprecedented unique collection illustrates how local people lived in one of the most prosperous cities in Europe. Children and young people also enjoy themselves here.

TIP Feniks: Reconstructing Flanders Fields

This details the story of Belgium's national recovery after the First World War. It is a story that transcends city and provincial boundaries, told from a human perspective. After all, the reconstruction was first and foremost the achievement of ordinary people.

7 March untill 15 November 2020
Grote Markt 34, Ypres
T. +32 57 23 92 20
www.inflandersfields.be

TIP Exhibition herSTELLINGEN (Reconstruction and Recovery) in the Yper Museum

'herSTELLINGEN' tells the story of the post-war recovery in the social-cultural sphere. Through eight different themes you will discover how the region picked up the threads of life after the First World War. There is a different theme each month, with related activities. Check the agenda!

21 March untill 17 January 2021
Grote Markt 34, Ypres
T. +32 57 23 92 20
www.ypermuseum.be

Menin Gate and Last Post

The Menin Gate is the most famous Commonwealth War Graves Commission's memorial in Flanders. It was designed in classical style by Sir Reginald Blomfield and stands on the site of one of the old town gates. Tens of thousands of soldiers passed through this gate on the way to the front, many of them never to return. The Menin Gate is maintained by the Commonwealth War Graves Commission (CWGC).
Every evening at 8 pm, a deeply moving ceremony takes place under the vast arch of the Menin Gate: the traffic stops and buglers from the Last Post Association and members of the local fire brigade play the Last Post. The ceremony began in 1928 and the buglers have performed it faithfully ever since, although they were banned from playing during the German occupation of 1940-44.

Menenstraat, Ypres
www.lastpost.be

Hooge Crater Museum

On the site of one of the fiercest battlefields of Ypres, and exactly opposite the 'CWGC Hooge Crater Cemetery', a unique First World War museum is housed in a restored church.

Meenseweg 467, Ypres
T. +32 57 46 84 46
www.hoogecrater.com

Entry Points Ypres Salient

You can discover the traces of the Great War along the front line of the Ypres Salient by exploring the local landscape in three entry points. In each entry point an illustrative film and info panels give you inside information on the war of that particular place. The cycle route Ypres Salient (35 km, departure on the Market Square Ypres leads you via the three entry points. The free digital app Ypres Salient shows you with aerial pictures the devastation of the war around Ypres. There are also several walking routes starting from the entry points.

Entry point North

This entry point gives information about surviving relics of the war on the north side of Ypres, such as *Yorkshire Trench*. The entry point is situated in *Klein Zwaanhof*, a reconstructed farm with typical regional characteristics.

Hoeve Klein Zwaanhof,
Kleine Poezelstraat 6, Boezinge

Entry point East

Entry point East is situated next to *Hooge Crater Museum*. This private war museum is housed in a rebuilt chapel, also once used as a school. Nearby, there is a renovated emergency home and the rebuilt castle belonging to the de Vinck family. The entry point offers information about the formation of the front in this sector.

Hooge Crater Museum,
Meenseweg 467, Zillebeke

Entry point South

Entry point South explores the fascinating wartime landscape around *The Bluff*, demonstrating how nature recovered following the depredations of the First World War.

Provinciedomein De Palingbeek,
Palingbeekstraat, Zillebeke

A SYMPHONY OF TREES, Ypres

Especially for the 2014-2018 centenary, Composer Piet Swerts created 'A Symphony of Trees' as homage to the City of Ypres and to Poet and Composer Ivor Gurney. This magnificent work, which concludes the Feniks project, will be performed by 'Koninklijke Harmonie Ypriana' (Royal Wind Band), which will be celebrating its own centenary in 2020.

24 & 25 october 2020,
Saint Martin's Cathedral Ypres

Feniks walk, Ypres

The Feniks walk takes you to all the most remarkable reconstruction sites in Ypres. Follow the circuit between the Colaertplein and the Market Square, passing some of the city's most outstanding buildings along the way.

Start: Station Ypres
The walk, including a number of fascinating 'did you knows' about the reconstruction, can be consulted free of charge via the app 'Ypres Salient 1914-1918: From the ashes'.

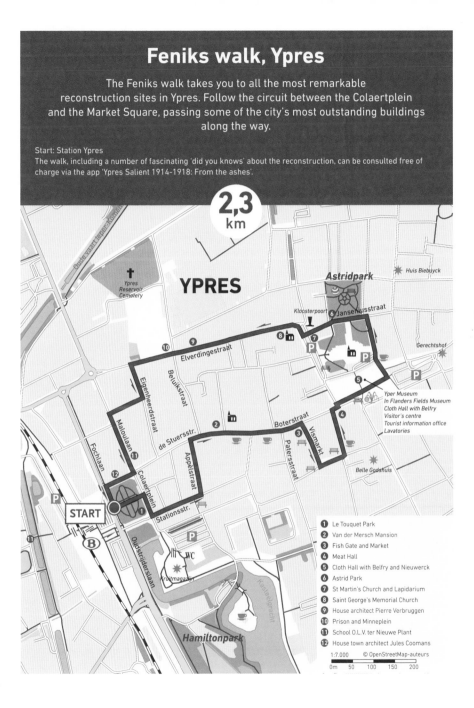

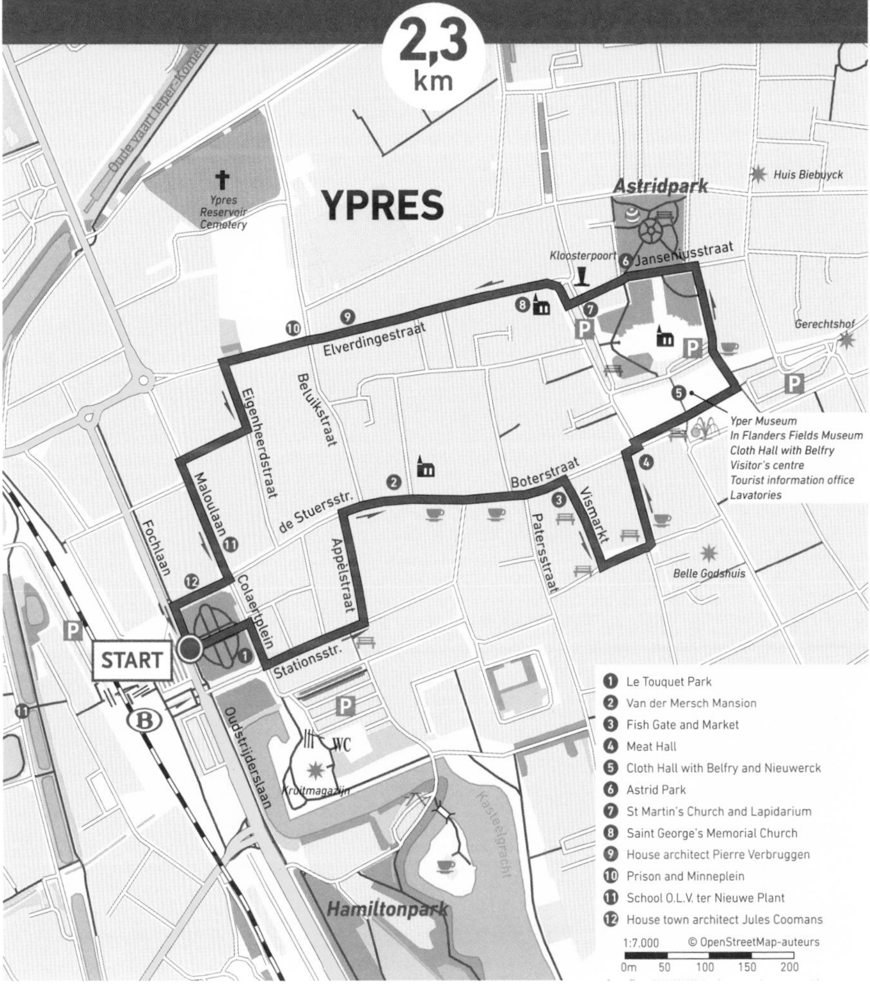

DIKSMUIDE

Middelkerke
Koekelare
Veurne
Diksmuide
Kortemark
ringem
Lo-
Reninge
Houthulst
Staden

Diksmuide rises from its ashes

Throughout history many cities have been completely destroyed by the violence of war. Names like Guernica, Oradour-sur-Glane, Dresden, Hiroshima and, more recently, Mosul are examples with which most of us will be familiar. It is more difficult to associate this kind of devastation with the Westhoek, which today is a peaceful oasis of calm and tranquillity. Even so, during the First World War dozens of towns and villages in the region were razed to the ground. One of the worst affected towns was Diksmuide, which found itself in the frontline for almost four years. The constant bombardments turned the city into a jumbled mass of ruins.

End 1918, Achiel van Sassenbrouck painting the ruins of Diksmuide.
Municipal Archive Bruges: Brusselle-Traen Collection)

When they saw the extent of the damage at the start of 1919, the press wrote that it would be impossible to rebuild Diksmuide in its original location. Not a single square metre had been spared from destruction by the war. However, plans to build a new town alongside the ruins of the old one proved to be premature. The first returning inhabitants took up residence in wooden huts close to the original town centre. During the first months and years, there was a serious shortage of living

Karel Focke, police commissioner for Diksmuide.
Municipal Archive Bruges: Brusselle-Traen Collection

“ From the diary of Karel Focke, police commissioner for Diksmuide (from 1909 to 1934)

On 22 November 1918, I returned to Diksmuide by train. For the first few days, I was able to live with a group of gendarmes in the cellars of the building once occupied by the Sisters of St. Nicholas. After that, I moved into a temporary military barracks on the Old Fish Market. I have very little in the way of possessions, but manage to get by. I clean my only shirt by boiling it in an iron pot. Fortunately, I am able to keep warm with an old stove I found in the ruins. I now sleep in a bed that once served the Germans and eat from an earthenware bowl that they probably used to feed their dogs. I have even adopted a German dog, which I have called Fritz. He is my sole companion, hunts rats and keeps away unsavoury characters at night.

accommodation, since the authorities were unprepared to face a challenge on such a massive scale.

Chickens donated by Queen Elizabeth of the Belgians.
(Municipal Archive Bruges: Brusselle-Traen Collection)

An unusual donation

Help can sometimes come from unexpected quarters and in unexpected forms. Queen Elizabeth raffled hens and chickens from her personal nursery to support the returning population. In July 1919, there was a draw among the returning farmers from Diksmuide, Oostkerke, Kaaskerke, Pervijze and Ramskapelle, with the lucky winners each receiving three royal chickens and one royal hen.

Commissioner Focke with daughter Madeleine and dog Fritz at their barrack on what is now the Vrijheidsplein.
Wilfried Beirnaert

Living in *drieduusters*

The infrastructure in the barrack districts was basic in the extreme. The roads were little more than pools of mud, there was no street lighting, no sewer system and an acute shortage of drinking water. In these circumstances, people were forced to fend for themselves. They took shelter in abandoned German bunkers from the war or knocked together rudimentary shacks with whatever they could find among the ruins. Later, the State paid everyone an allowance of 3,000 Belgian francs (equivalent now to roughly 3,900 euros) for the purchase of materials to build their own temporary homes. This 'emergency housing' sprang up everywhere in the Westhoek, and was known locally as *drieduusters*, after the local dialect word for three thousand. Various humanitarian aid organisations helped to relieve the worst of the suffering. In the summer of 1919, the American Commission for Relief in Belgium opened a store in Diksmuide, where returning refugees could buy household items, food, clothes, shoes, etc. at low prices.

State assistance and the use of prisoners-of-war for the reconstruction

The city authorities were faced with a colossal, almost impossible task. Like many devastated towns, Diksmuide was unable to meet the cost of the reconstruction unaided. Since its own financial resources were inadequate, the town allowed itself to be 'adopted' by the Belgian State, which Endeavoured to fund the repair of all public property. Prisoners-of-war were drafted in to clear up the ruins. This work was later taken over by ordinary labourers. Once most of the roads had been made clear, work started in March 1919 on the removal of debris and the demolition of German observation towers. The statistics relating to this clearance work were staggering:

20.000 m³
of concrete was broken up

195.000 m³
of earth was moved
to re-level the ground

3.000 tons
of shells and shrapnel
were recovered as scrap iron

16 million
stones

3.000 tons
of iron

35.000 m³
of rubble

6.000 m³
of firewood

were recuperated from the battlefields
and used for the reconstruction of the city

Stones were collected for use in the reconstruction of the town.
Municipal Archive Bruges: Brusselle-Traen Collection

Architect Jos Viérin drew up the general plan for the reconstruction of the town.

It was only in 1922 that the immense task of demolition, clearance and rebuilding was completed.

A traditional street plan in preference to a new ring road

Although the reconstruction could only start after the Armistice, preparations were made while the war was still in progress. In 1916, Diksmuide town council held a meeting in Paris to discuss the post-war reconstruction of the town with Brussels architect Charles Patris. Patris had already made a design, which prioritised traffic circulation, public hygiene and the aesthetics of the town's streets and squares. He also foresaw a ring road around the town centre. However, Patris's wartime plan was little more than a series of preliminary sketches and it was rejected by the Department for the

St. John's Hospital in Diksmuide, designed by architect Charles Patris.
Municipal Archive Diksmuide

Devastated Regions after the Armistice. The department then appointed Jos Viérin to draw up a new plan. As a consolation prize, Patris was allowed to design the town's new St. John's Hospital.

'Oud Vlaenderen'

Architect Jos Viérin was appointed to draw up a general plan for the reconstruction. With only a fewer minor adjustments, such as the widening of the roads to take account of an increased traffic flow, this plan closely reflected the pre-war

In an emergency... live on a boat!

The first returning residents who registered with the civil registry in 1919 gave a very strange address as their 'place of abode'. Because there was almost no housing available, some families lived in boats and barges moored on the River Yser. Their vessels often had impressive-sounding names like *Comte de Flandre, Duc de Brabant, Fils Unique, St.-Antonius, Martha*, etc., and often offered accommodation for two couples and their children.

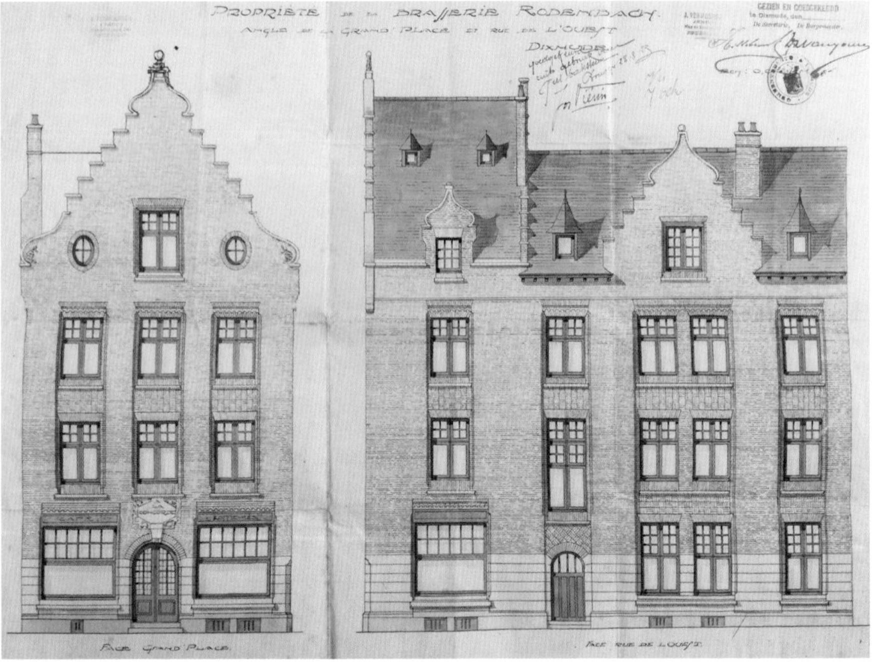

Presentation drawing, Brasserie A la Concorde, 1923.
Municipal Archive Diksmuide

pattern of streets. The choice of Viérin determined to a large extent the way Diksmuide still looks today. He supervised the stylistic uniformity of the rebuilding and issued guidelines to other architects who were active in the town. Nothing could be built without his approval. Viérin opted resolutely for a historicising reconstruction, dominated by a neo-Flemish Renaissance style. The reasoning behind this decision was not purely aesthetic, but also ideological. By harking back to the building tradition of the 15th and 16th century, he wished to project an idealised image of Flanders' 'Golden Age'. In the Westhoek, historicising brick architecture with Late-Gothic and Renaissance elements goes hand in hand with stepped gables, rounded arches, imposing roofs and the typical yellow brickwork of the region.

The town expands

At the start of the 1920s, houses began to spring out of the ground like mushrooms. The new Diksmuide was soon bursting at the seams. There was scarcely enough room to cram in all the building projects that people wished to

The Market Square, 1923. Work on the church and the town hall in progress.
Municipal Archive Diksmuide

implement. As a result, it was decided to expand the town's boundaries. Esen ceded 100 hectares of its territory to Diksmuide, which more or less doubled in size. This new piece of ground was the site for De Pluimen, one of the many garden estates built in the region after the war. Even the old city park was divided up to create additional plots for building.

View of the De Pluimen garden estate.
Municipal Archive Diksmuide

While the reconstruction of the majority of private buildings was completed within a few years after the Armistice, it was not until 1923 that serious work could begin on public property.

A poster for the first post-war fair.
Municipal Archive Diksmuide

The approval of the plans for the setting of the new building line resulted in heated discussions between the town authorities and the Department for the Devastated Regions. These plans were vital for the reconstruction programme, since they fixed the boundaries between private land and public land, and therefore determined where people were free to build and where not. The straightening and widening of the streets and squares made necessary the compulsory purchase of some private land. In this context, the officials of the Department for the Devastated Regions were more inclined to set the building line with practical and aesthetic considerations in mind, whereas the local politicians in Diksmuide were more concerned about the complaints of their voters. These tensions slowed down the progress of the reconstruction. The most striking example occurred in 1923, when the council ordered work on its own town hall to be stopped, because the Department for the Devastated Regions' work site did not comply with the building line that had been agreed.

People make a town

As the number of returning refugees increased, the city gradually began to live again. If the speed of the reconstruction was remarkable, so too was the resilience of the local population. The weekly market resumed as early as February 1919. This required a degree of improvisation, since large parts of the old Market Square were still covered with ruins. Even so, it did not take very long before people from the surrounding villages found their way to Diksmuide each Monday to buy butter and eggs from the local farmers. In July 1920, the first fair and district festivities were held. Clubs and societies started up again. Cycling competitions and horse races were organised. The schools reopened in 1920. The carnival returned in the spring of 1923 and in

New town and village centres

A desire to preserve the past and a political reluctance to compulsorily purchase land meant that plans for radical change were pushed to one side. As a result, there are very few 'new' town or village centres in the Westhoek. The only exceptions were the villages of Oostkerke, Kaaskerke and Sint-Joris, all of them on the banks of the Yser, where a new orientation or a new location was chosen for their reconstruction.

Rededication of the Sint-Veerle Church, Oostkerke 1923.
Westhoek verbeeldt, privécollectie

October of that year the first official football match took place. As the number of completed new houses increased during the 1920s, so the population of Diksmuide systematically grew. Before the war the town had 3,884 inhabitants. By the start of 1920, this number had fallen to around 450, but by the end of that same year (according to the ten-yearly census held on 31 December) it had already risen again to 1,113. Nevertheless, it would not be until 1961 that the pre-1914 figure was equalled. Following the inauguration of the new town hall in 1925, the pace of reconstruction slackened off, although work on a number of other iconic buildings was still in progress. It was also in that year that the Belgian State's 'adoption' of Diksmuide came to an end. There was still much to do, but so much had already been accomplished. The battlefield tourists who ploughed their way through rubble-filled streets in 1919 would have found a town reborn, if they had taken the trouble to return just six years later.

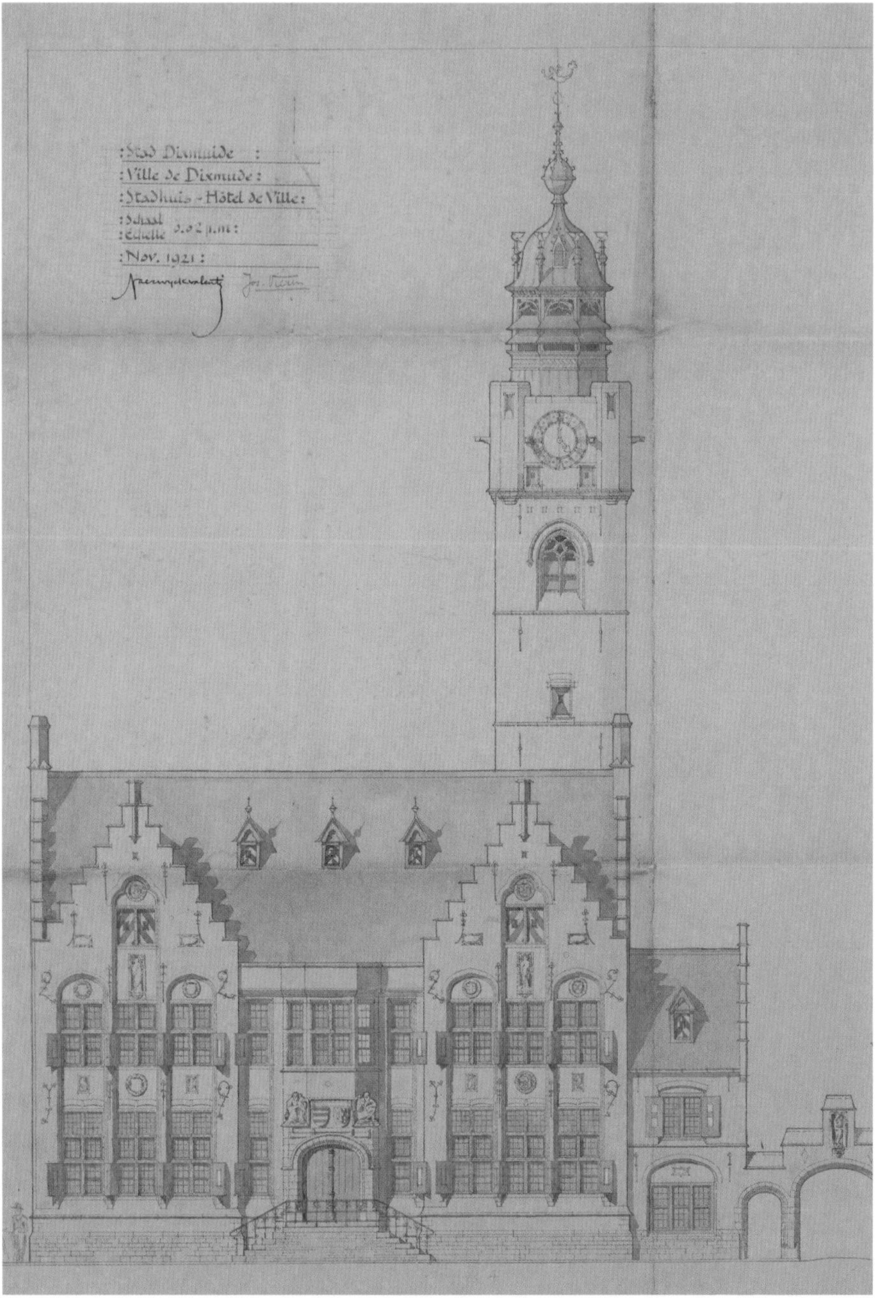

Jos Viérin and Valentin Vaerwyck, presentation drawing for the reconstruction of the town hall.
Viérin Archive.

TIP

Exhibition 'Risen from the ashes'

This temporary multimedia exhibition shows how the town resurrected itself after the war. Witnesses who were there will guide visitors through the ruins of the town and tell stories of the reconstruction based on their own experience.

Grote Markt 6, Diksmuide
Ingang via Dienst Toerisme
T. +32 51 79 30 50
www.bezoekdiksmuide.be

TIP

Show: 'Risen from the Ashes' on the Market Square in Diksmuide

On Wednesday, 20 May 2020, the town of Diksmuide is organising a large scale event on the Market Square. With music, theatre and humour, scenarist Bart Cafmeyer tells stories great and small from the reconstruction period in a lighthearted manner, complete with live music and spectacular projections.

For more info:
Free. Everyone welcome!
www.bezoekdiksmuide.be
www.flandersfields.be/nl/feniks2020

Yser Tower, Gate of Peace and Yser Crypt

The first Yser Tower was built in the 1930s, as a memorial to the Flemish soldiers who had died at the front, which ran along the line of the River Yser between 1914 and 1918. During the Second World War, the site was the scene of various German-Flemish ceremonies. This original tower was destroyed by an explosion in 1946 and it was not until 1965 that a new structure arose, phoenix-like, from its ashes. In recent years, the tower has also housed a museum. The Museum on the Yser tells the story of the Belgian-German front during the First World War, using the memoirs of soldiers, civilians and refugees on both sides of the line. In addition to a magnificent view over the old battlefields of the Yser Front, the 84 metre-high tower also offers fine panoramas of Diksmuide and the Westhoek.

IJzerdijk 49, Diksmuide
T. +32 51 50 02 86

The Trench of Death

This kilometre-long network of revetments, saps and dug-outs was one of the most dangerous Belgian positions on the Western front, situated just 50m from a German bunker.

IJzerdijk 65, Diksmuide

O.-L.-Vrouwhoekje Stuivekenskerke (Our Lady's Corner)

Our Lady's Corner (O.-L.-Vrouwhoekje) in Stuivekenskerke is located between Nieuwpoort and Diksmuide. The church tower was an important Belgian outpost during the war, and its preserved ruins contain an orientation table which highlights key places of interest on the Yser Front. The adjacent chapel of remembrance is ringed by memorial stones to units of the Belgian Army which served near here. There is also an original demarcation stone, with the inscription: 'Here the invader was brought to a halt...' The nearby railway embankment still contains dugouts and other interesting relics from the war years. This embankment marked the Belgian front line for much of the period 1914 -1918.

Always open, free entrance

German military cemetery, Vladslo

The German military cemetery at Vladslo is the last resting place of Peter Kollwitz, a young student volunteer who was just 17 years of age when he was killed in October 1914. Deeply affected by her son's death, Käthe Kollwitz created her world-famous sculpture 'The Grieving Parents'. 25,645 German soldiers are buried here. Käthe Kollwitz was a famous expressionist artist from Berlin. Her work was considered to be an example of Entartete Kunst (perverted art) by the Nazis and was removed from most museums and public buildings. Her grandson Peter was killed on the Eastern Front in 1942. Surprisingly, the sculpture survived the Nazi occupation of Belgium during Second World War.

Houtlandstraat 3,
Vladslo

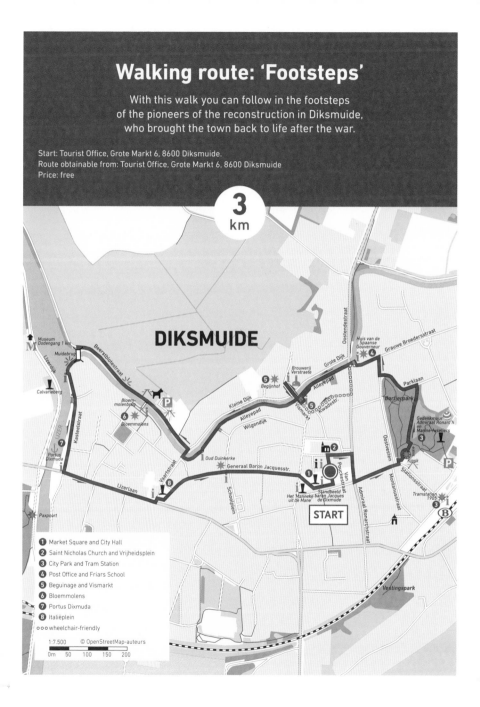

Walking route: 'Footsteps'

With this walk you can follow in the footsteps of the pioneers of the reconstruction in Diksmuide, who brought the town back to life after the war.

Start: Tourist Office, Grote Markt 6, 8600 Diksmuide.
Route obtainable from: Tourist Office, Grote Markt 6, 8600 Diksmuide
Price: free

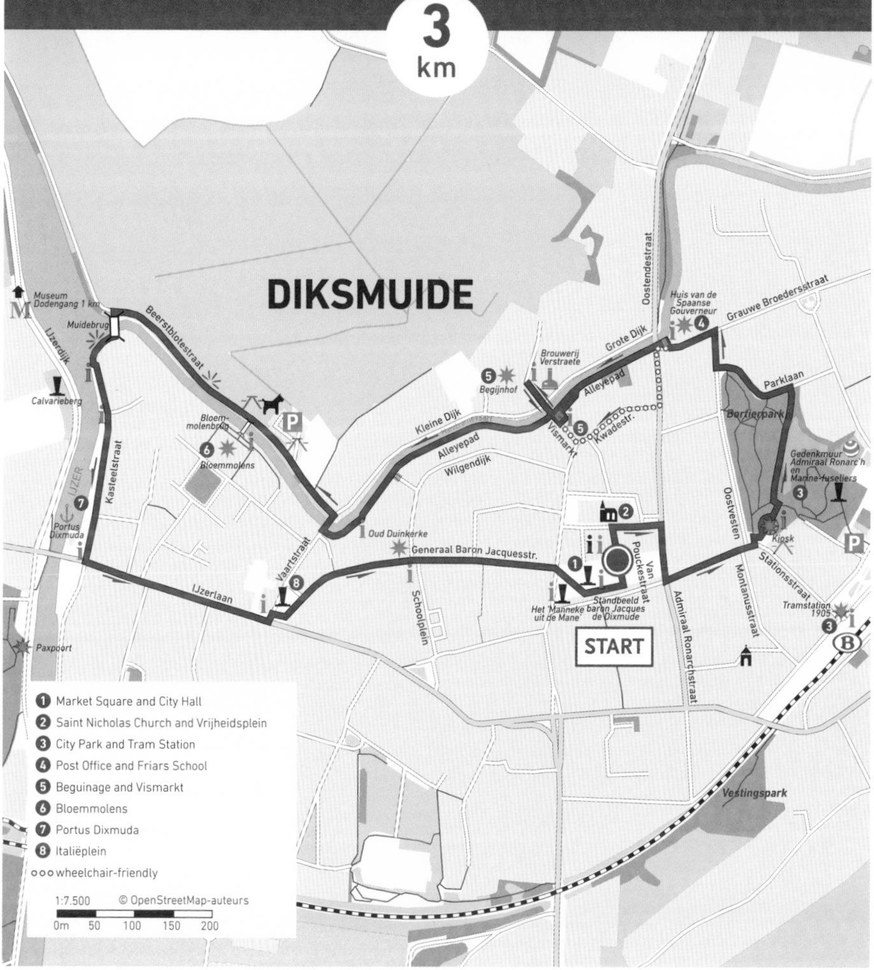

NIEUWPOORT

Middelkerke
Koksijde
Nieuwpoort
De Panne
Veurne
Diksmuide
Alveringem
Lo-
Reninge
Houthulst

Follow the Feniks

Today, Nieuwpoort is a thriving coastal resort, but in the 19th century it was still very much the same impoverished polder village it had been in the Middle Ages. Fishing was the only real source of income for its few hundred inhabitants. Lack of resources made major change impossible.

An uninhabitable ruin...

During the First World War, Nieuwpoort found itself right on the frontline. After four years of constant bombardment, almost nothing remained of the town. As early as 1916 it had been described as 'an uninhabitable ruin'. By the time the German troops withdrew, Nieuwpoort had been virtually razed to the ground.

View of the cloth hall in Nieuwpoort
Brusselle-Traen Collection

As with Ypres and Diksmuide, it was at first doubted after the Armistice if Nieuwpoort could be rebuilt on its original site. Some voices suggested that a new location might be better, but the return of the town's pre-war inhabitants soon settled the matter. It was decided to reconstruct the town on the Yser estuary.

A difficult return

The returning refugees lived in cellars or constructed rudimentary shelters from what they found in the ruins. To prevent this improvised building from getting out of control, the town council decided to allocate the old city park for the accommodation of its returning citizens. The King Albert Fund (KAF), which was under the jurisdiction of the Ministry of the Interior, promised to provide emergency housing that it would lease to returnees. But these barracks were slow to arrive.

View of the barrack town
Walter Lelièvre Collection

By the summer of 1919 there were hundreds of families on the waiting list for accommodation, but the necessary work had still not been completed by the end of the year. To ease the problem, the town made available public land on the Arsenaalplein and along the Willem De Roolaan for people who were in a position to erect their own hut. It was not until the start of 1920 that the displaced persons were finally able to move in to the new barrack district.

A barrack district with full public facilities

The plans for the barrack district were drawn up by architect Jos Viérin. By the time he had finished, it was actually more like a mini-town than a district. Two parallel main streets ran alongside each other, meeting at a square in the middle of the site. Along each street there were two rows of 'houses'. Each house had its own garden, where the residents could grow vegetables. In addition to a temporary town hall, a church and a post office, there were also a boy's and girl's school, an orphanage and a field hospital. In fact, the barrack town had public facilities that many towns undamaged by the war might envy. Even so, living there was far from easy. The 'houses' were wooden huts with tin roofs, which were freezing cold in

Clearing away the ruins
Walter Lelièvre collection

the winter and boiling hot in the summer.

The accommodation crisis

It was not just the former inhabitants of Nieuwpoort who came to live in the barracks. People from other parts of the country also found their way there. These so-called 'Easterners' came from the areas of Belgium that had been occupied by the Germans during the war. They were now attracted to the Westhoek by the prospect of work during the process of reconstruction. Many of them never returned to their original homes.
The ever increasing stream of returning refugees and other newcomers made it necessary for the authorities to also install barracks in Nieuwpoort-Bad, which at that time was part of the municipality of Oostduinkerke. The King Albert Fund found it impossible to cope with this growing demand for accommodation. The fund was only able to erect 9,000 huts, whereas there was a need for tens of thousands throughout the front region. In an effort to ease the crisis, the national government decided to pay an allowance of 3,000 francs to people who were willing and able to build their own emergency home. It was only from 1921 onwards, by which time the reconstruction was well under way, that the demand for barracks started to decline.

Emiel Coppieters (° 1849 – † 1922)

Emiel Coppieters (° 1849 – † 1922) was a socialist politician from Ghent. He sat in the Senate from 1908 until his death and was also an alderman in his home city. Coppieters was a building contractor by profession and before the war implemented a number of major public works projects at locations that included the canal at Charleroi and the harbours at Ostend, Bruges, Ghent, Antwerp and Brussels. His wide experience of waterways, in combination with his important political connections, made Coppieters the ideal man to lead the reconstruction work in the coastal region. With this in mind, he was appointed as High Royal Commissioner for the region in 1919. In Nieuwpoort he supervised the work on the locks and the harbour, and also played an important role in the rebuilding of the town.

At the start of 1923, the KAF began removing barracks from Nieuwpoort for use elsewhere, although it was not until the 1950s that the last huts finally disappeared.

The new town plan

Like many towns and villages along the old frontline, Nieuwpoort was unable to bear the cost of the necessary reconstruction work from its own resources. In 1919, it became one of the municipalities 'adopted' by the Belgian State. These municipalities came under the supervision of the Department for the Devastated Regions. Led by a High Royal Commissioner, the department organised and funded the rebuilding of public property, in return for which it had far-reaching powers and control over the municipal finances. Reconstruction of the coastal region was entrusted to Emiel Coppieters. Architect Jos Viérin was appointed to draw up a new town plan for Nieuwpoort and to supervise the reconstruction of the most important public buildings. This was not a chance appointment. As the provincial architect-inspector, he had worked before the war on the restoration of historical buildings in the town. In 1906, he had also made a study for the redevelopment of the market square.

Work on the locks.
Walter Lelièvre Collection

When designing his plan, Viérin (a native of Bruges) adopted a dual approach. In the town centre, he opted resolutely for a historicising reconstruction, which largely preserved the pre-war street pattern. Some roads were widened to comply with relevant hygiene and traffic requirements, but that was as far as his changes went. However, to the south of the town he foresaw a zone for new and more modern expansion.

'Vieux-neuf'

During the reconstruction process, most towns and cities opted to employ a regional style: the Brabant style in Leuven, the Meuse style in Liege, and the Flemish Renaissance style (a combination of Neo-Gothic and Renaissance) in the Westhoek and along the coast. The reconstruction was

Work on the locks.
Walter Lelièvre Collection

Reconstruction of the market square.
Walter Lelièvre Collection

expected to reconcile the 'old' with the 'new' by identifying the 'Old Flanders' that had been so strongly in evidence at the World Exhibition held in Ghent in 1913. In this way, the reconstruction was intended to project the image of Flanders' 'Golden Century', showing that Flanders would rise from its ashes stronger than ever before. The reconstruction of the town was the ideal opportunity for Viérin to implement his 1906 study. His focus was on the core of the town. The Cloth Hall, the Church of Our Lady, St. Bernard's College and a number of private houses were carefully rebuilt to their pre-war design. In the immediate vicinity of the market square he insisted on the artistic reconstruction of buildings in the prevailing regional style, so as to maintain stylistic unity in this part of the town. He also expected this to serve as an aesthetic example for other private buildings that would be constructed around the town centre. With this in mind, he supervised and approved the plans of all the other architects active in Nieuwpoort. Plans that did not conform to his ideal historical image were rejected.

The 'garden district' concept

The post-war reconstruction offered opportunities to experiment with new visions for urban development. One of the most important of these innovations

The construction of private buildings in full swing, 1923.
Walter Lelièvre Collection

in Belgium was the introduction of the English concept of the 'garden district'. This was an attempt to remove people from the lower social classes from impoverished and sub-standard terraced housing in working class areas to more comfortable housing with common social facilities and utilities in a green environment, in which public hygiene and the aesthetics of the streetscape played an important role.
Raphael Verwilghen, director of the Building Directorate for the Devastated Regions first encountered this new concept during a study trip to the United Kingdom. On his return to Belgium, he argued for the introduction of the concept during the reconstruction process. The first such garden district was created in Roeselare, the town where Verwilghen was born. The work began in 1919 and it was named as the *Batavia District* in honour of the Netherlands, where many Belgian refugees, including some from Roeselare, had fled during the war. The streets in the district were named after the towns where refugees from Roeselare had been given shelter.
The construction of the garden district in Nieuwpoort began in 1920. The design, drawn up in collaboration with Raphael Verwilghen, was made by the Brussels architect Albert Van Huffel (most well-known for

Reconstructing the 'Recollettenstraat' in Nieuwpoort.
Walter Lelièvre Collection

the Koekelberg Basilica). Similar garden districts were also created in Diksmuide and Ypres and were often the first residential areas to be completed in the war-devastated towns.

Forced adjustments

The reconstruction of Nieuwpoort did not always proceed as smoothly as expected. Viérin's general plan needed to combine the conflicting interests of different official bodies, but these bodies – the town council, the Roads and Bridges Agency, the Department for the Devastated Regions, the National Rail Service, etc. – seldom took due account of each other's projects.
The interference of national politics served only to complicate matters further. In June 1920, Minister of the Interior Renkin resigned and was replaced by Henri Jaspart, who had a very different vision of the reconstruction process. He was keen to make budgetary savings, one of which was to cancel the provision that had been foreseen for the necessary compulsory purchase of the ground in Nieuwpoort that was needed to make Viérin's plan possible. As a result, the architect was forced to make amendments, cutting back the building line to a strict minimum. Consequently, it was only necessary to compulsorily purchase land at the quay and around the market square, paid for by the town. Plans to straighten and widen roads were also abandoned, so that the town's medieval street plan was largely preserved.
It took until February 1921 before Viérin's general plan was approved, but after that things moved quickly. By the end of 1923 the majority of private buildings had been completed or were under construction.

Work on the locks.
Walter Lelièvre Collection

TIP 'Follow the Feniks' show

'Follow the Feniks' promises to be a memorable show with video-mapping, theatre and live music on the Market Square in Nieuwpoort. It tells a moving story about letting go, taking back and moving on. Directors Mieke Dobbels and Frieda Vanslembrouck, ably supported by musician Johan Bouttery, highlight the aspects that make Nieuwpoort a typical 'reconstructed' town - or how something was made from nothing. An original evening walk, with surprising anecdotes and a dramatic finale that will live long in the memory!

Every evening from 29/07 to 2/08/2020.
Nocturne walk from 19.00.
Reservation required.
Finale on the Market Square at 22.00.
Free entry.

Westfront Nieuwpoort

In the autumn of 2014, the new 'Westfront' visitors centre was opened close to the historic complex of locks known as the 'Ganzepoot' (Goose Foot). The centre's permanent exhibition explains the importance of the Nieuwpoort locks and their role in the flooding of the Yser plain during the First World War. Temporary exhibitions, nocturnes and workshops explore other related themes.

Kustweg 2, Nieuwpoort
T. +32 58 23 07 33
www.westfrontnieuwpoort.be

Clics, a do-exhibition – 'Building at the front'

Westfront Nieuwpoort
from 1/07 to 30/09/2020

Exhibition: 'My War' - Juul Filliaert, 1914-1918 Journalist, publisher, collector

In the Westfront Visitors Centre in Nieuwpoort the war years of Juul Filliaert are brought back to life. As the editorial secretary of the front newspaper *De Belgische Standaard*, he was closely involved in all the initiatives taken to meet the cultural and social needs of the soldiers in the trenches. His personal archive, with documents and a unique collection of works by wartime artists, will give this prominent witness of the war the attention he has long deserved.
To mark this exhibition, a richly documented book about the wartime experiences of Juul Filliaert will be published.
The exhibition and the book have both been developed by Luc Filliaert, the grandson of Juul Filliaert.

Exhibition runs from 8/5/20 untill the end of the year.

Follow the Feniks /Feniks 2020 Nieuwpoort

Follow the Phoenix through the historic town centre of Nieuwpoort.

Start: Westfront Nieuwpoort
Route obtainable from :
Tourist Office in Nieuwpoort-Stad, Marktplein 7, 8620 Nieuwpoort or
Tourist Office in Nieuwpoort-Bad, Hendrikaplein 11, 8620 Nieuwpoort

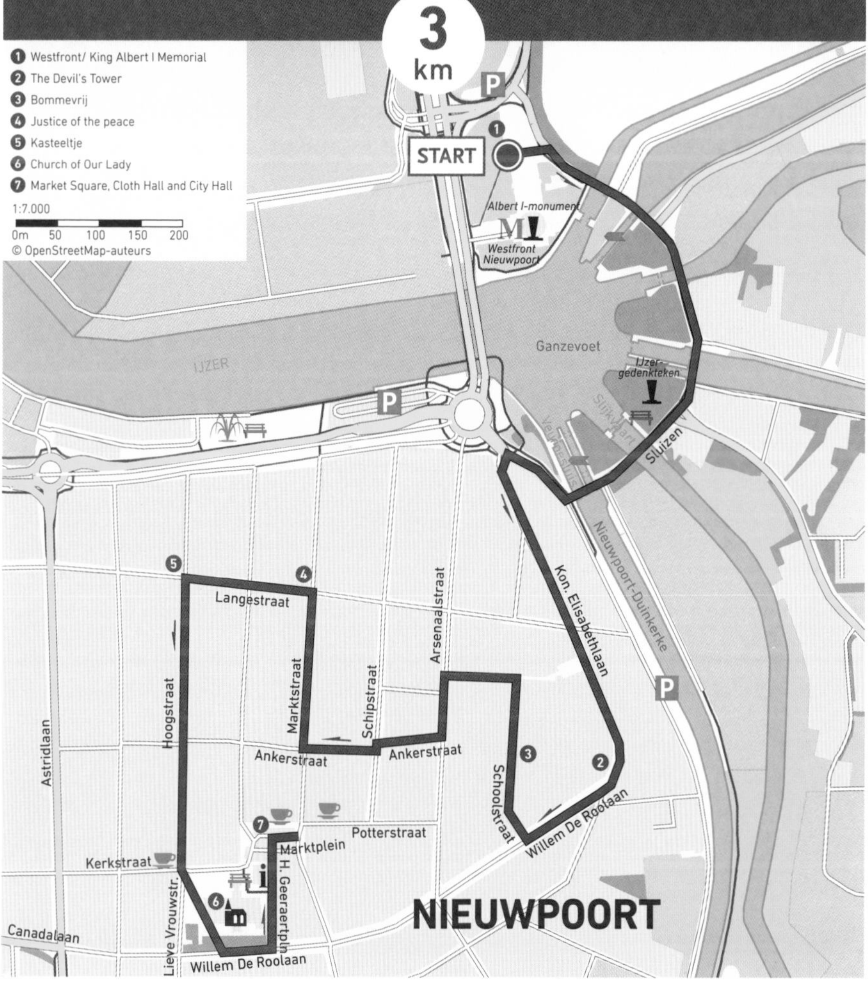

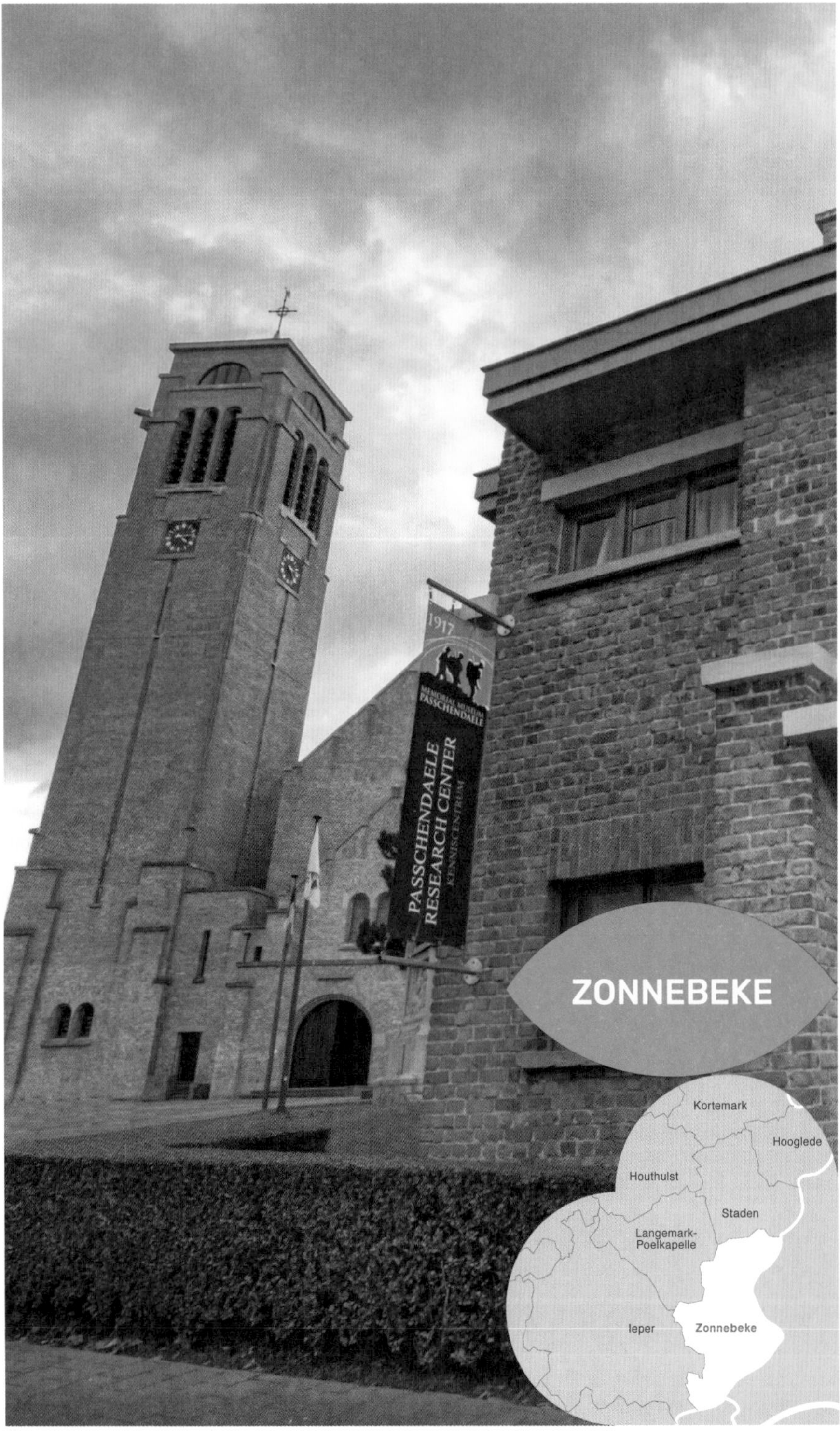
1917
MEMORIAL MUSEUM
PASSCHENDAELE
PASSCHENDAELE
RESEARCH CENTER
KENNISCENTRUM

ZONNEBEKE

Kortemark
Hooglede
Houthulst
Staden
Langemark-
Poelkapelle
Ieper
Zonnebeke

Huib Hoste introduces modernism in the Westhoek

In the old front region you can hardly find any buildings that date from before the First World War. Everything was destroyed, as result of which the current visual appearance of the Westhoek is determined primarily by the homogeneity of the architecture that was used for the post-war reconstruction. Within the context of this reconstruction, architect *Huib Hoste* was a unique exception. Even though the original inhabitants of the ruined towns and villages wanted a return to the past as a way to wipe out all traces of the war, Hoste was nevertheless able to design and build a number of unique modernist gems.

“ From the diary of Huib Hoste

'We saw more houses which, either by ill fortune or from old age, had fallen into ruin. In our mind's eye we have imagined such piles of ruins and believed that in this way we knew what the ravaged cities must look like... I have thought more and more about the death of things, created by men's hands, and lo, it is all much worse than we thought; so bad, in fact, that nature can no longer take her normal course and finds her eternal power has been paralysed.'

Report of Huib Hoste's fourteen-day cycle tour through the Devastated Regions, *De Telegraaf*, 7 December 1918

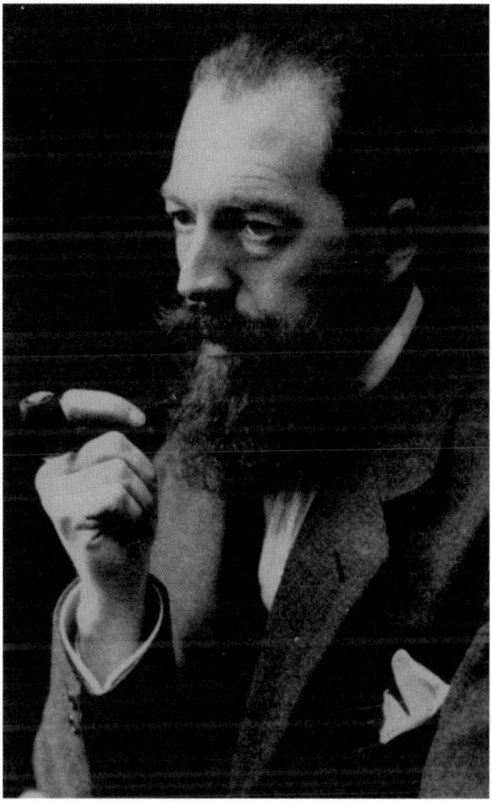

Huib Hoste, 1922
Zonnebeke History Society

Traditionalist versus modernist thinking

From 1914 onwards, even though the war had only just started, politicians and architects began to discuss the nature that the post-war reconstruction should take. This debate was essentially a clash of opinions between the 'traditionalists' and the 'modernists'. Traditionalists wanted to rebuild the towns and villages in such a manner that their historic appearance was restored, preferably through the use of existing regional architectural characteristics. Behind this 'traditional' outer shell, they were happy to use modern building techniques to meet contemporary needs and norms. The modernists rejected this approach. Why? In their vision, these traditionalist buildings would never offer viewers and residents the same aesthetic experience as the original medieval buildings, with their worn-down steps and weather-beaten sculpturing. The modernists also had ethical objections to the traditionalist approach to history. A reconstruction based on the pre-war

Mission Dhuicque

In May 1915, the Brussels architect Eugène Dhuicque was appointed to lead the 'Mission du Ministère des Sciences et des Arts'. This team was tasked with photographing and recording all buildings of historical and cultural significance in unoccupied Belgium, and with rescuing as many artistic treasures as possible. After the war Dhuicque was an important opponent of an identical reconstruction. He believed that each age has its day and that an identical reconstruction was therefore a falsification of history. Ironically, the documentation collected by his mission was in important factor in making a traditional reconstruction possible.

The Belgian Monument in Amersfoort, 2017: a monument to express the gratitude of Belgian refugees to the people of the Netherlands, designed by Huib Hoste.
MMP1917

model would attempt to create a historical continuity that no longer existed after the war. It was the traditionalist vision that eventually prevailed. The reconstruction became identified with regionalism: a reconstruction *à l'identique*.

A new structural language

Huib Hoste – born in Bruges in 1881 as Hubert Hoste - was a pioneer of modernism. His architectural designs during his formative years displayed Neo-Gothic and eclectic influences, but Hoste became increasingly fascinated by Dutch modernist architecture. During the war he fled to the Netherlands, where he designed the Belgian Monument in Amersfoort. Huib Hoste introduced cubist forms and new materials, such as glass, steel and concrete, into Belgian architecture.

The design plan for the church at Zonnebeke, with amendments added, 1921-1922.
Zonnebeke History Society

The rebuilding of the church in Zonnebeke, 1924.
Zonnebeke History Society

The rebuilding of the church in Zonnebeke, 1923.
Zonnebeke History Society

Huib Hoste and the Church of Our Lady in Zonnebeke

'The reconstruction had to be speeded up, so it was decided to appoint an architect for groups of two or three municipalities. I was allocated, amongst others, Zonnebeke, with its young "frontline priest". He asked me to build a new church to replace the one that had been completely destroyed. It had to be a Romanesque church, he said. "In other words, with thick walls and sparse openings?" I asked. "No, a church with rounded arches, " he replied. My design was approved by the bishopric and I won't reveal how we managed to get around all the various commissions. I gave the priest his church with rounded arches, and also with a reinforced concrete roof, visible in the interior, and a tower alongside the church, etc. The priest wasn't very happy with the end result. He had a somewhat banal boundary wall built around the church instead of the one I had designed, and, with the exception of the high altar, had all the interior furnishing designed and implemented by others in a completely different style. Even so, many priests who also needed a new church came to visit Zonnebeke, praising it to the heavens and saying that they wanted one just like it... But then they gave the task to others.'

Why the church in Geluveld does not look like its original design

Not everyone was open for the new ideas of modernism. In an exchange of letters between Huib Hoste and Pastor Delrue of Geluveld, it is clear that the two men disagreed strongly. Hoste was very pleased with his own work: 'So you don't like your new church? Well, as far as I am concerned – and that is something that doesn't happen very often – I am delighted with it. It will be a beautiful and atmospheric space to the honour and glory of God. And that sleek tower with the little windows of the baptismal chapel at the bottom! It is a joy to behold!' As time passed, Pastor Delrue became increasingly dissatisfied: 'We asked you to build a Gothic church; in other words, Flemish Gothic, like you can see everywhere in our region. Here, as in other places, you have just stuck to your own opinion and given us something with cubism. What's worse, it is Dutch cubism! No, this is unacceptable. We, the senior figures in the village, do not want a second Zonnebeke. We want a triangular choir, a portal and front gable with three large windows, a tower with a point and not a brick-kiln, and a nave not a barn, not even from the outside.'

Even after many adjustments, Hoste's plan was eventually rejected. The design of the church in Geluveld was taken over by Jules Coomans, the city architect of Ypres.

The design plan for the church at Geluveld, 1921.
Zonnebeke History Society.

The design plan by Huib Hoste for the town hall in Zonnebeke, 1921.
Zonnebeke History Society

Around the billiard table in the Sint-Hubert, 1922-1924. Huib Hoste and Sylvie Carpentier are seated.
Daniël Hoflack

Huib Hoste becomes an urbanist architect

From 1919 onwards, towns and villages that had been completely destroyed during the war were eligible for 'adoption' by the Belgian State for the purpose of their reconstruction. Seventy-one of the ninety-five municipalities in the Westhoek chose to be adopted in this manner by the newly established Department for the Devastated Regions. This meant that their reconstruction was effectively in the hands of the department, rather than the municipalities themselves. The budget for the necessary work and the basic design and building line plans were approved by the High Commission for the Reconstruction. Huib Hoste was appointed as an urbanist architect for a number of municipalities, including Zonnebeke and Geluwe.

Emmanuel Iweins, owner of the Chateau, the second inhabitant in Zonnebeke, 1919.
Zonnebeke Historical Society

TIP

Huib Hoste and modernism

As soon as you enter the church in Zonnebeke, you also enter into a dialogue with Huib Hoste. You will discover why the Church of Our Lady is now regarded as the very first modernist church in Belgium and will also be able to see what other plans Hoste had for buildings in our region. A pair of VR-glasses allows you to see the church as the master-architect originally intended, while a 3D-visualisation of the first years after the war takes you back through time to the Zonnebeke of the early 1920s.

Church of Our Lady
(Onze-Lieve-Vrouwkerk)
Roeselarestraat 1, Zonnebeke
T. +32 51 77 04 41
info@passchendaele.be
www.passchendaele.be
The exhibition runs from 18 April to 15 November 2020
Open daily from 09.00-17.00, last admittance at 16.00
Free entry

Zonnebeke church tower

Climb the tower and discover how the history of the region has changed the landscape in the exhibition 'A Scarred Landscape'. The climb will reward you with a phenomenal view over the surrounding countryside.

Roeselarestraat, Zonnebeke

Memorial Museum Passchendaele 1917

The MMP1917 not only brings to life the Battle of Passchendaele but is also located in a chateau reconstructed after the Armistice. Built in the typical 'Iweins style', the chateau stands in its own magnificent park in the heart of Zonnebeke. You can also visit one of the original emergency barracks provided by America after the war.

Berten Pilstraat 5A, Zonnebeke
T. +32 51 77 04 41
www.passchendaele.be

CWGC Tyne Cot Cemetery and visitors centre

With almost 12,000 graves and 35,000 names on its memorial to the missing, Tyne Cot Cemetery is the largest Commonwealth War Graves Commission military cemetery in the world, a silent witness to the Battle of Passchendaele. The visitors centre provides further information about what happened here and offers a fine panoramic view over the battlefields of 1917.

Vijfwegestraat,
Passendale (Zonnebeke)

Polygon Wood

A beautiful and serene wood, with several commemorative sites for Australian and New Zealand soldiers who died during the First World War.

Lange Dreve,
Zonnebeke

The Old Cheese Factory (De Oude Kaasmakerij)

Discover how refugees returning after the war set up a flourishing cheese-making business in an old potato cellar.

's Graventafelstraat 48 A,
Passendale (Zonnebeke)
www.deoudekaasmakerij.be

Walking route: 'Zonnebeke reborn'

A new heritage walk - 'Zonnebeke reborn: what after the Great War?' - forms part of the series 'Stories for along the way' and tells the story of how life and society in Zonnebeke recovered after the First World War.

Start: Zonnebeke Castle
The route brochure can be purchased in the shop at the Memorial Museum Passchendaele 1917, Berten Pilstraat 5A, Zonnebeke
Price: 5 euros

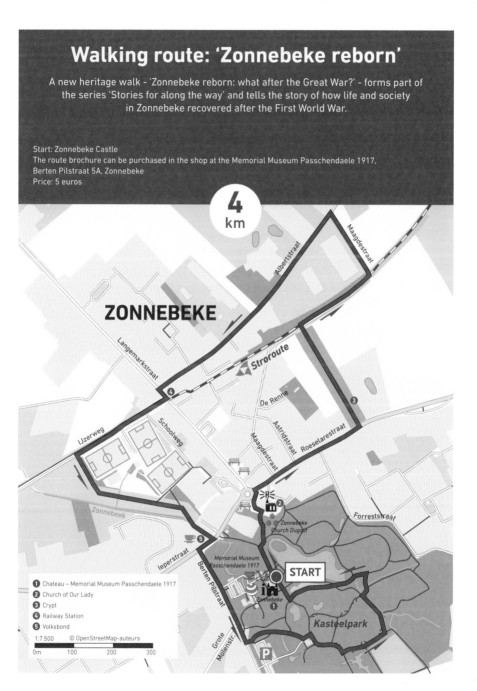

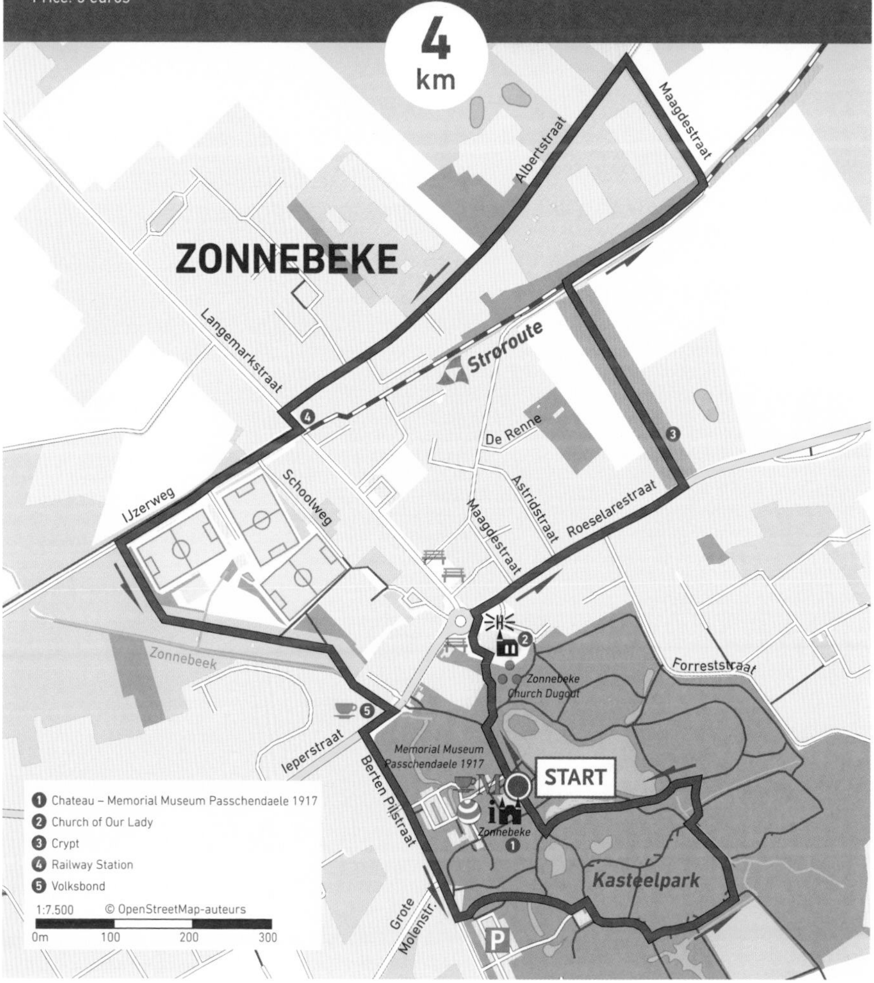

HEUVELLAND

The Feniks in Heuvelland

The rich natural beauty of the West Flanders hill country – Heuvelland – was already attracting many visitors even before the First World War. In particular, there were various flourishing tourist activities on or around the Kemmelberg (Mount Kemmel). Above all, there was a magnificent view over the surrounding countryside from the wooden belvedere (complete with bear cage!) on top of the hill. After the war people continued to visit, but now to search for the last resting place of their loved ones. During this same period, the local inhabitants gradually began to return to their ruined homes.

Café Pax, with the temporary barrack village and the Kemmelberg in the background.

Café Pax returns to the West Flanders hills

In March 2020, the legendary 'Café Pax' will be 'reborn' in the Heuvelland Visitors Centre. This tavern with its symbolically significant name was the one of the first to reopen its doors in Kemmel after the Armistice. Taverns and inns played an important role in helping to repair the social fabric of society during the reconstruction period. It was here over a quiet drink that people exchanged news and gossip about what was happening in the region. The taverns and inns also had an increasingly important tourist function as the 1920s progressed.

As this 1970s photo shows, the belvedere still towers above the village from its lofty perch on the Kemmelberg.
'Westhoek verbeeldt', private collection

Jules Arnout (1901 – 1988)

Jules Arnout was born and bred in Kemmel. Even when the war came dangerously close in the autumn of 1914, the young Jules, together with his parents and his seven brothers and sisters, continued to live in the village, from where they could hear the sound of the guns at the front. When heavy fighting broke out to the south of Ypres in 1915, the family fled to the neighbouring village of De Klijte. During this flight, Jules' mother and his one-year-old brother were killed. As the front continued to move forward, so the family withdrew further towards France. After the war, they returned to Kemmel, where Jules worked in his father's battlefield clearance team.

1919 as 'year zero'

For Kemmel, 1919 was the new year zero. The *Spring Offensive* of 1918 had wiped the village off the map. As soon as the guns finally fell silent, the first villagers started to return. There were many others who could not face the idea of a life among the ruins and decided to remain in the countryside, where they had sought shelter during the war. Their place was gradually taken by 'Easterners', who moved here from other parts of Flanders further to the east. These newcomers sometimes took over land that had originally belonged to others, which often led to conflict. But in spite of this influx, Kemmel's population never returned to its pre-war level. Even today – like many other municipalities in the Westhoek – there are fewer inhabitants than in 1914.

The team led by Cyrille Arnout (far right, without shovel), with Jules Arnout (fifth from the right).
'Westhoek verbeeldt', private collection

Roads as lifelines

Without transport, it was impossible to survive in the devastated front region, never mind rebuild houses. To bring in the required food supplies and building materials, it was first necessary to repair the roads. Local authorities employed teams of labourers to restore the main traffic arteries. Usable roads were also important for the growing number of tourists, since they often had motor cars, which were becoming increasingly popular in the 1920s. It was not without good reason that Café Pax also had a petrol pump!

Julie Catrysse (1901 – 1988)

When the Great War broke out in 1914, 13-year-old Julie Catrysse was living with her parents in Aartrijke, a village near Bruges. This was in the Etappengebiet, a zone of German occupation not far behind the front. After the war, the family decided to move to the Westhoek, where there were jobs and money to be earned during the reconstruction. The Catrysses finally settled in Kemmel, having walked from Ypres, where they arrived by train. They lived in a self-made barrack and father Catrysse soon found work as a brickmaker. Julie worked as a barmaid in Café Pax.

Marshal Foch visits Kemmel on 21 May 1921. The standard of the Flemish Veterans of Kemmel is flying proudly in the centre of the picture, behind the entrance portal of the ruined parish church.

Fauna and flora

The First World War was a disaster for the biodiversity on and around the Kemmelberg. When the Brussels botanist Jean Massart made an analysis of the biological value of the front region in 1919, he came to a sad conclusion: 'There are only a few minor traces of felling woods [...]; the mature woods that once covered the flanks of the Kemmelberg have disappeared entirely.' The region's fauna and flora only recovered slowly and with difficulty. The relatively isolated location made it hard for the lost species to re-establish themselves. In comparison with the pre-war situation, the number of different species remained limited. Even so, the Kemmelberg continued to be a popular destination for walkers and cyclists. In 1926, a new stone belvedere was erected on the site of the original wooden one, and is a typical example of reconstruction architecture in the Heuvelland region.

Marshal Foch visits

On 22 May 1921, the French Marshal Foch visited Kemmel, accompanied by various Belgian dignitaries. It was during this visit that the standard of the Flemish Veterans of Kemmel was dedicated. Following the celebration of mass in St. Lawrence's Church by the Bishop of Bruges, a large crowd of people made their way to the top of the Kemmelberg, where it was announced that a monument to the French fallen would be built,

The Warande Castle, gateway to the nature reserve was rebuilt in 1925 by the Mayor of Kemmel and is now the administration centre for the municipality.

although it would take until 1932 before this was finally erected.

Hotel Delobel – Het Labyrint

One of the hotels where tourists could spend the night in Kemmel in the 1920s was the Hotel Delobel. The building, with its typical bay-windowed tower under a tent roof, was inspired by the architectural style that was popular at the time on the Belgian coast. The name was later changed to 'Het Labyrint', a reference to the maze that stood at the edge of the castle park. The maze was cleared to make room for the expansion of the village after the Second World War, but was recreated in 1987.

Gustave Bruneel (1863 – 1932)

Gustave Bruneel was not only a baron and the lord of the local manor, but for almost 25 years he was mayor of Kemmel, a senator and a provincial counsellor. As a major landowner, he represented the interests of the agricultural sector. He was a leading figure in the reconstruction process. His vision for the future of 'his' village was one that foresaw modern houses of the same type, in keeping with the 'garden district' concept that was starting to come into fashion (see p. 44). The present-day Kasteeldreef, leading to his old castle, is still lined with these typical 'workers' houses from the 1920s.

Dumoulin pipe factory
'Westhoek verbeeldt', private collection

Dumoulin pipe factory

Joseph Dumoulin was one of the many entrepreneurs who saw interesting commercial opportunities in the reconstruction of the Westhoek's towns and villages. Originally from Rumbeke, after the Armistice he moved to the Devastated Regions, where he started a brickworks in Langemark and a brick and pipe factory in Wijtschate. His pipes were not only used for the new sewers, but also for the repair of drainage systems damaged in the war. Joseph Dumoulin's pipe factory enjoyed a golden period in the years immediately after the war, but was finally forced to close in 1975.

TIP

Expo 'CAFE PAX. The return to the West Flanders hills'

With Café Pax, the atmosphere of life in the temporary housing of the post-war period is brought back to life. The attic floor of the visitors centre will be transformed into a barrack tavern in which local villagers will guide you through the region as it was in the years immediately after the First World War. It was not just the local community that recovered quickly; tourists also soon found their way back to the hill country in the south-west of the Westhoek. Visitors, returnees and newcomers: they all met at Café Pax!

Heuvelland Visitors Centre

Visitors' Centre Het Heuvelland

The exhibition 'Landscape and War. The Heuvelland 1914-1918' illustrates the influence of the hills on the course of the First World War. The traces that you still find in the landscape today are discussed in detail too.

Sint-Laurentiusplein 1, Kemmel
T. +32 57 45 04 55
www.toerismeheuvelland.be

The Pool of Peace, Wijtschate

The Pool of Peace (or Lone Tree Crater) in Wijtschate is a now peaceful reminder of the great Mine Battle of 1917. On 7 June 1917, the British attempted to capture Messines Ridge, a strategically important area of high ground around the villages of Wijtschate and Mesen (Messines). The opening of the offensive was marked by the detonation of 19 deep mines under the German lines between Ploegsteert and Hill 60. The explosions formed enormous craters in the landscape. The largest and most impressive crater is the Pool of Peace. It is 12 metres deep and has a diameter of 129 metres. The site is administered by the provincial government of West Flanders.

Permanent free access,
from sunrise to sunset.

Kruisstraat, Wijtschate
T. +32 57 45 04 55

Bayernwald, Wijtschate

This site occupies an elevation of 40 m: strategically interesting to keep an eye on the enemy and, where necessary, to react. Ypres is 6 km away as the crow flies. After a fierce battle, the site fell into the hands of the Germans who renamed the place 'Bayernwald' and expanded it into a large, invincible fortress. Here you get (which is unique) the story of the Mine Battle from the German point of view. Today's Bayernwald is a faithful reconstruction of 320 m of trenches, four bunkers and two mine shafts. The site is also accessible to wheelchair users on a walking path along the trenches.

Tickets: Visitor centre Het Heuvelland
Address Bayernwald: Voormezelestraat near Croonaert Wood, Wijtschate
T. +32 57 45 04 55

French monument, Kemmel

On the summit of Mount Kemmel there is an impressive French memorial which commemorates the heavy fighting that took place here in April 1918. The memorial is known popularly as 'The Angel'.

Kemmelbergweg, Kemmel

French military cemetery, Kemmel

(French ossuary)
The French mass grave is located on the western flank of the Kemmelberg, with a view of the Zwarteberg, Rodeberg and Scherpenberg. The beautiful view also gives immediate insight into the strategic importance of this sector and of the Battle of the Kemmelberg. The mass grave (actually, four mass graves) were not built until after the armistice of November 1918. Today, 5,294 French soldiers lie buried here. Only 57 could be identified, some only partially. Their names are indicated on the memorial to the fallen, the obelisk made of white natural stone with a Gallic cockerel at the top, which rises in the centre of the mass grave.
The site is accessible to wheelchair users.

Kemmelbergweg 19, Kemmel

POPERINGE

Feniks: children of the reconstruction

During the First World War, Reningelst was just a few kilometres behind the front. The village was surrounded by military camps, training grounds, stables and workshops. A narrow-gauge railway ran through the centre of the village, making it an easy-to-spot target for enemy planes. As a result, there were frequent bombardments. Even so, most of the villagers did not move away. The brewer continued to brew his beer and the baker baked his bread. However, from 1917 onwards the severity of the bombardments increased and in the spring of 1918 Reningelst suffered great hardship and serious damage.

“ Pastor Van Walleghem

14 April 1918
'... One of the heaviest bombardments I have ever experienced. No fewer than 65 shells fell all around us. After it is over, we go outside. The village square is in a terrible state and there are six large shell craters in the cemetery.'

16 April 1918
'Two-thirds of the population have already fled. In spite of the pain of leaving behind their homes and all their possessions, most are putting on a brave face. On every side you can see cattle being herded towards Poperinge and Abele in droves. People don't really know what to make of the situation or what to do.'

On 18 April, orders were issued that the village must be evacuated. When the villagers later returned, they found that it had suffered considerable damage. On 11 January 1919, Pastor Van Walleghem journeyed from Dikkebus to De Klijte, where he reported the vicarage to be damaged 'but repairable'. While he was there, he met two Chinese playing a piano in a ruined house. Travelling via Westouter, he arrived back at the vicarage in Reningelst, where he visited a group of nuns who had just returned. 'Reningelst is better than Westouter; at least parts of it can be repaired.'

The ruin of the Six family's Sint-Joris (St. George's) brewery and malt house.
Photo Mission Dhuique. KIK-IRPA

The Department for the Devastated Regions 'adopted' Reningelst, the only village in the Greater Poperinge region to be given this status. This meant that financial assistance was available to build temporary homes or to repair damaged houses and property. As early as January 1919, the widow Van Cayseele was awarded compensation of 250 francs for damage caused to her land by the laying of the railway. Filling and levelling a four-metre wide shell hole merited compensation of 10 francs. Payments were also made for the demolition and removal of the wartime stables. Farmers received compensation for cut down trees (elms) and smashed hedges. War orphans were given proper recognition and war pensions

“ Margriet Six

During the war, my father, Nestor, remained in his brewery in the village. My mother, Marie-Elodie, was pregnant with me and fled with her three oldest children to Lichtervelde, where I was born on 7 November 1914. We couldn't let my father know because Lichtervelde was in the area occupied by the Germans, so it was impossible to contact him. He only saw me for the first time after the war. In 1917, he was also forced to flee as a refugee, to Calvados in France.

In 1919 our family was finally reunited in Reningelst. Because our house at the brewery was completely destroyed, we moved into the inn on the corner of the street. The brewery itself was damaged, but was soon back in working order. And so I made my first acquaintance with brewing and a brewer's life.

The ruins of the Six family's Sint-Joris (St. George's) brewery and malt house, with the damaged St. Vedastus church in the background. *Photo Mission Dhuicque. KIK-IRPA*

The Six family in the 1920s; Margriet is standing on the right.
Mark Adriaen

were agreed and paid. Slowly but surely, people began to get back on their feet and resume a more normal life.

The Poperinge architect François Van Welden made a design for our new house. The architectural style was eclectic, but with some clear Norman influences. The house was built in yellow brick and the family was able to take up residence in September 1923. Alongside the house my father had a chapel built, dedicated out of gratitude to Our Lady. Sadly, he died just ten years later. The four children helped mother to further run the brewery and malt house with success.

Even today, the house and the chapel still dominate the village square in Reningelst.

St. George's brewery after its reconstruction.

TIP

Expo: 'Feniks – Children during the Reconstruction'

The story of Margriet Six is one of the central elements in this exhibition. Children, teenagers and young adults talk to the visitors and tell them how they experienced the years after the war. What did Margriet think when she was finally able to decorate her own room in the rebuilt brewery? How did the fifteen-year-old Ernest react when his father, a well-digger, dug up the corpse of a French soldier and had to give everyone present a slug of gin, to help them recover? What hopes did Florent Houwen have when he set off to teacher training college and was he ever able to fulfil his dreams?

This exhibition will run from 4 July 2020 in an iconic location: the malt house tower in the old St. George's brewery.

Viewing platform

The old malt house has a viewing platform that offers a fantastic panorama of the village, the valley of the Grote Beek and the West Flanders hills.

The malt house tower

The history of the village brewery dates back to the 17th century. In 1907, it was purchased by Nestor Six from his grandmother, Octavie Camerlynck. Three years after this new start, Nestor won a gold medal for his beer at the World Exhibition in Brussels. Immediately before the war, he carried out a number of expansion works and during the early years of the conflict the brewery worked at full capacity, since the demand for beer was huge. It was only in March 1917 that it became too dangerous to continue production. The site was damaged during the remaining fighting, but Nestor Six soon had his business up and running again after the Armistice. Following his death in 1933, his widow and children kept the brewery going and eventually grew it into a sizeable company, where the last beer was finally brewed in 1963. The site was given protected status in 1997 and since 2012 has been home to the Kid's Brewery, a place bursting with fun-packed activity for young and old alike.

The malt house tower survived the First World War, but later fell into disrepair after the closure of the brewery and finally collapsed in 2001. It was restored in 2018-2019 as part of the Horizon 2025 programme, a provincial project that aims to transform new and existing towers into attractive viewing platforms.

Kid's Brewery, Reningelstplein.
Reningelstplein, Reningelst

Kama in Reningelst

During the exhibition, everyone will be given the chance to contribute their own drawing to the new design of Feniks street. Imagine a row of houses where a gap suddenly appears, because one of them has been flattened by a shell. How would you fill in this space? Budding illustrators are free to express their ideas - and one of them is Kamagurka.

But Kama will also take things a stage further, by knocking on the doors of local people's homes to ask them what they think. Do they like his design? Would they rebuild or not? If not, what would they do instead? The result of 'Kama in Reningelst' can be viewed as a documentary within the exhibition, in a room where the creative 'brews' of locals and visitors gradually ferment into a new village street.

Lijssenthoek - Visitors Centre

CWGC Lijssenthoek Military Cemetery is the largest First World War hospital cemetery. It contains the graves of almost 11,000 soldiers, most of whom died in the evacuation hospital that was located in the fields nearby. The hospital continued to be active after the Armistice and German prisoners-of-war and Chinese labourers were treated here until October 1920. Many of them died during the Spanish flu epidemic.

Boescheepseweg 35A,
Poperinge
www.lijssenthoek.be

TALBOT HOUSE

Talbot House

During the First World War, this elegant townhouse was transformed into an Everyman's Club. In December 1915, in the centre of unoccupied Poperinge, the army chaplains Neville Talbot and Philip 'Tubby' Clayton decided to create a place where soldiers could spend time when they were out of the trenches. For three years, their club was a haven of rest and relaxation for thousands of Allied troops, irrespective of rank. Today, as then, Talbot House is a peaceful stop on the Great War trail that leads through the Westhoek. The exhibition 'The Pilgrim's Way' – about the first post-war pilgrimages to the battlefields and the British military cemeteries – will continue in the Garden Room until May 2020.

Gasthuisstraat 43, Poperinge
museum and guest house
www.talbothouse.be

Memorial site at Busseboom

Busseboom is the location of the only monument in Flanders that commemorates the service of the Chinese labourers during the First World War. The site is also an ideal stopping point for cyclists and walkers, where they can enjoy a brief rest while reading the information panels that tell this remarkable Great War story.

Corner Visserijmolenstraat 18 –
St.-Jansstraat, Poperinge
admittance free

DE LOVIE
Alveringem
Lo-
Reninge
Vleteren
Poperinge
Ieper

Health care after the First World War

Before the First World War, there were dozens of private castles in the Westhoek. The peaceful wooded plain around Ypres was a haven of tranquillity, where the wealthy gentry of the region liked to spend their leisure time in magnificent country estates. The largest of these estates was *De Lovie*, on the boundary between Poperinge and Proven. The castle was built in 1856 by *Marie Josephine Beatrix Cornelie van Renynghe* as a summer residence for her son, *Julius Karolus Cornelius Van Merris*. Although the war destroyed many of the castles that were nearer to the frontline, De Lovie remained intact, since it was far enough behind the trenches to be out of range of the German guns. As a result, it served as a British and French headquarters.

In the early 1920s, the castle was bought by the Sint-Idesbald Sanatorium (with the financial support of the Province of West Flanders) as a centre for the care of tuberculosis patients. Because antibiotics were only widely available after the Second World War, the treatment of the disease in the inter-war period consisted of not much more than rest, a healthy diet and plenty of fresh air, all of which were available in the quiet and sylvan surroundings of the sanatorium.

The interior of the doctor's office in the sanatorium.
'Westhoek verbeeldt', private collection

First taking care of the towns, then taking care of people

Health care in Belgium underwent many changes in the years after the First World War. Whereas the policy before 1914 focused primarily on the practice of curative medicine and the prevention of epidemics. After the Armistice the government wished to invest more heavily in measures to improve the general health of the population. New medical discoveries led to new insights and greater attention for a more focused form of health care. During the 19th century, major efforts were made to clean up the towns by implementing large-scale sanitation projects to improve general living conditions, but after the war the priority was switched to treating the individual. This new approach was based on the principle of subsidised freedom of choice. The government did not organise health care itself, but contracted private organisations to provide it in return for financial support. This resulted in the development of private (Catholic) hospitals and care homes alongside municipal facilities. It was not until 1936 that the first Belgian Ministry of Health was set up.

A poster in the fight against tuberculosis.
Amsab

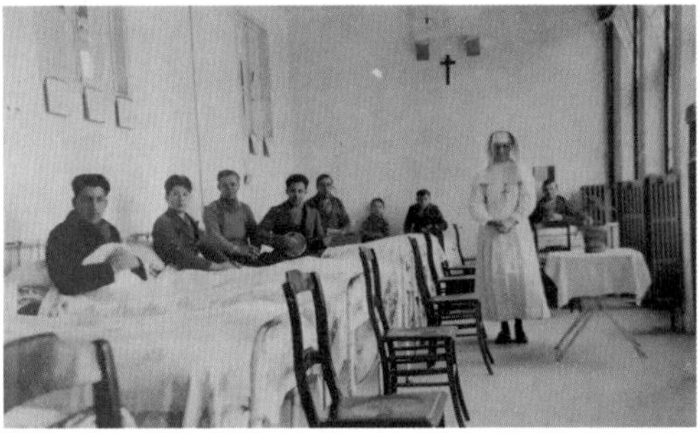
The ward for tuberculosis patients in the sanatorium.
De Lovie vzw

The fight against tuberculosis

During the First World War, people did not only die as a result of the fighting. In occupied Belgium, the number of fatalities from tuberculosis doubled during the war years, largely as a result of poor diet and lack of food, which wore down the body's natural resistance. For this reason, the National Food and Aid Committee decided to launch a campaign specifically designed to combat TB, as it was commonly known.
The positive experience of these wartime measures led

De Lovie today

De Lovie vzw is a social non-profit organisation that provides support to children, young people and adults with a cognitive or other limitation. In addition to the castle, the organisation is active at some 25 other sites in the Westhoek.

to the foundation in 1929 of the National Association for the Combating of Tuberculosis, which united the most important private initiatives under a single banner. This brought large sections of the population into direct contact with medical personnel and health care institutions for the very first time. The Sint-Idesbald Sanatorium was also affiliated to the National Association for the Combating of Tuberculosis.

The Lourdes grotto at De Lovie

In order to give comfort and support to its patients, in 1933 the sanatorium's board of administration decided to construct a Lourdes grotto in the castle grounds. This was a clear indication of the board's essentially Catholic approach. The grotto can still be visited today.

From barracks to castle

The sanatorium had its origins as a field hospital set up by the Belgian Army at Houtem (near Veurne) in 1916. After the war, the sanatorium was opened for ordinary citizens. The original accommodation – a wooden hut – was transferred to De Lovie around 1930. The hut has recently been restored and can still be seen in the castle park.

COME AND VISIT DE LOVIE

TIP

Exhibition: 'Tuberculosis after the First World War'

The exhibition tells the personal stories of patients, medical staff and their families, as well as illustrating the impact that the disease had on the sufferers and their environment. At the same time, you can also visit the magnificent castle park.

De Lovie Castle
Krombeekseweg 82, Poperinge
T. +32 57 334 965
info@delovie.be
www.delovie.be
The exhibition runs from 25 April to 15 October 2020
Hours of opening:
Wednesday to Sunday, 11.00 to 17.30
Admission free

De Lovie as a hub

During the war, De Lovie was an important hub behind the Allied frontlines. In addition to being a headquarters, various railway lines ran through the park, one of the first aerodromes was located nearby and there was also a prisoner-of-war camp. The casualty clearing station known as 'Dozinghem' (dosing them) was just down the road and the graves of those who died can still be visited in the large military cemetery of the same name.

LANGEMARK - POELKAPELLE

Kortemark
Hoogled
Houthulst
Staden
Langemark-Poelkapelle
Ieper
Zonnebeke
11·SEPTEMBRE·1917
SUR·CE·COIN·DE·TERRE·BELGE
RAVAGÉ·PAR·LA·GUERRE·TOMBA·POUR
LA·DÉFENSE·DU·DROIT·VIOLÉ
UN·HÉROS·FRANÇAIS·GEORGES·GUYNEMER
DONT·LES·AILES·VICTORIEUSES·CONQUIRENT
A·VINGT·ANS·UNE·GLOIRE·INCOMPARABLE
DANS·LE·CIEL·DES·COMBATS·LES·AVIATEURS
BELGES·QUI·EURENT·L'HONNEUR
DE·LUTTER·A·SES·COTÉS·ONT·ÉLEVÉ·CE
MONUMENT·EN·TÉMOIGNAGE·DE·LEUR
ADMIRATION·NÉE·DE·LA
FRATERNITÉ·DES·ARMES
8·JUILLET·1923

The Poelkapelle tank and other stories

During the early years of the war, Poelkapelle (Poelcapelle) escaped serious damage. This all changed in 1917, when the village found itself in the eye of the storm. The British offensive towards Roeselare developed into a battle of attrition, during which Poelkapelle was completely destroyed.

When the first inhabitants returned to the village after the Armistice, all they found was a sign to indicate where it had once stood and, nearby, the wreck of a British tank sunk deep in the mud.

Poelkapelle shortly after the end of the First World War. The sign board is the only way of telling that a village once stood here. *Bruges Municipal Archive: Brusselle-Traen Collection*

The shell-damaged carcass of a British tank.
Michel Gheeraert Collection

Penny children and tourists fraternise at the wreck of the British tank in 1926. *Het Geheugen van Nederland: Spaarnestad Photo Collection*

The penny children

The tank became a tourist attraction, which testified to the terrible fighting that took place here. The children who played around the tank soon came to be known as penny children, from the coins they received from the generous British tourists. The tank was removed by the occupying Germans in 1941.

King Albert I welcomes Woodrow Wilson at the station in Adinkerke.
NARA

The Stationsstraat in 1923. Reconstruction work is in full swing. Temporary barracks are being replaced by permanent homes. In the distance, the Guynemer Monument is still in scaffolding.
Michel Gheeraert Collection

Tabula rasa

As the population grew, a barrack village was built between the station and the old village centre. This location was not chosen by chance. The station was the main supply hub, where an old German narrow gauge railway brought in much needed building materials. Initially, it was suggested to move the position of the new Poelkapelle village closer to the station, but this was not possible because the barracks were now in the way. As a result, the idea was dropped.

Missing out on a V.I.P. visit

When the American president Woodrow Wilson visited the old front region in June 1919, it was planned that he would also stop at Poelkapelle. But it never happened. The signpost marking the village's location had fallen over and the American convoy drove straight past it...

The marriage portrait of Jules and Godelieve Rosselle in France.
Guido Degraeve Collection

Godelieve Vanwildemeersch: La Belle Rosselle

During the First World War my families fled as refugees to Brittany. When we returned to Poelkapelle, life was nothing more than ruins, clearing up and farming. As the eldest daughter, it was up to me to repair the clothes of our large family and I also did the family shopping. This meant going once each week to Roeselare on foot: thirty kilometres there and back! When my fiancé Jules Rosselle decided to move to France, I didn't hesitate to follow him. We got married and started a farm at Chaumont-le-Bois. I wasn't the only girl who left the Westhoek in search of a better life.

The people of Poelkapelle took the opportunity presented by the reconstruction to enhance their village with wider streets, more open spaces and a new market square. In 1923, the new church and the prestigious Guynemer Monument were inaugurated. This monument commemorates the French ace George Guynemer, who died near the village in 1917.

TIP

Exhibition and walk

In Poelkapelle, the Feniks cycle route (see p. 91) focuses on how law and order was re-established in Belgium's 'Wild West'. The village is also the starting point for a walk that includes testimonies from people who returned after war.

German military cemetery

This sombreness is very much in evidence at the German military cemetery - 'Deutscher Soldatenfriedhof' - in Langemark. However, its powerful simplicity lends a poignant air to this haunting burial ground. Behind the monumental entrance building in pink Weserberg sandstone lie 44,304 soldiers, 24,917 of them in a mass grave. Over 600 cadets and student volunteers, serving in the 22nd - 27th Reserve Corps, are amongst the dead. They were killed in October 1914 during futile attempts to break through in the direction of Ypres. For this reason, the cemetery is also known as the 'Studentenfriedhof '. The sculpture of four bronze soldiers by the Munich sculptor Emil Krieger seems to reflect the sorrow of these bleak statistics.

Klerkenstraat 86A, Langemark

The Brooding Soldier

The Canadian Forces Memorial at Sint-Juliaan was erected in remembrance of the 2,000 dead of the First Canadian Division, who were killed in the fighting which followed the German gas attack of 22 April 1915. The monument dates from 1921 and was designed by F.C. Clemeshaw. It is also known as 'The Brooding Soldier' - a reference to the grieving Canadian warrior, his head bowed in sorrow and his hands resting on the butt of his upturned rifle. It is generally regarded as one of the most poignant military memorials in the Salient. The Brooding Soldier is maintained by the Commonwealth War Graves Commission (CWGC) and managed by Veterans Affairs Canada.

Crossroads Brugseweg-Zonnebekestraat, Sint-Juliaan

Guynemer Monument and pavilion

The impressive French memorial is the monument to French fighter pilot Georges Guynemer. Guynemer is undoubtedly one of the pioneers of war aviation. In 1916 and 1917, the airspace above Poelkapelle was also the theatre of heroic air battles. Guynemer had taken off near Dunkirk on 11 September 1917 but disappeared without trace after a flight over Poelkapelle. His body was never recovered. The monument to Guynemer was inaugurated on 8 July 1923. It is crowned by a graceful stork, which refers to the 'Escadrille des Cigognes', a squadron of the French Air Force.

The new Guynemer Pavilion alongside the story of Guynemer also provides information about other pilots and the tactics and technology of aviation during the First World War. The replica of Guynemer's plane, the Morane-Saulnier, is the real eye-catcher.

Guynemerplein, Poelkapelle

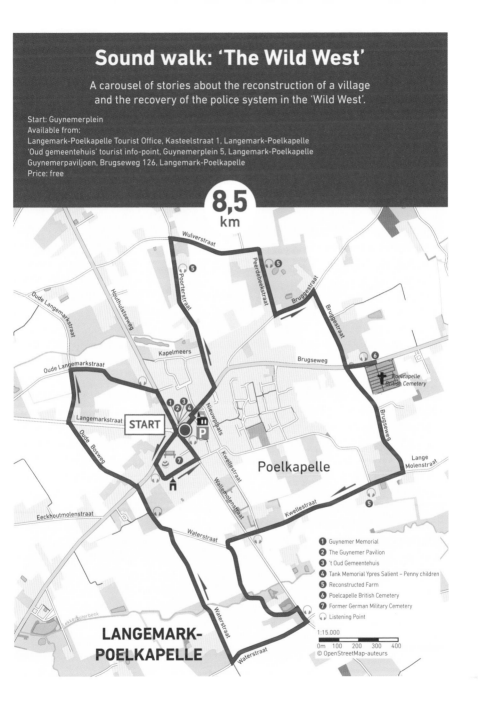

Sound walk: 'The Wild West'

A carousel of stories about the reconstruction of a village and the recovery of the police system in the 'Wild West'.

Start: Guynemerplein
Available from:
Langemark-Poelkapelle Tourist Office, Kasteelstraat 1, Langemark-Poelkapelle
'Oud gemeentehuis' tourist info-point, Guynemerplein 5, Langemark-Poelkapelle
Guynemerpaviljoen, Brugseweg 126, Langemark-Poelkapelle
Price: free

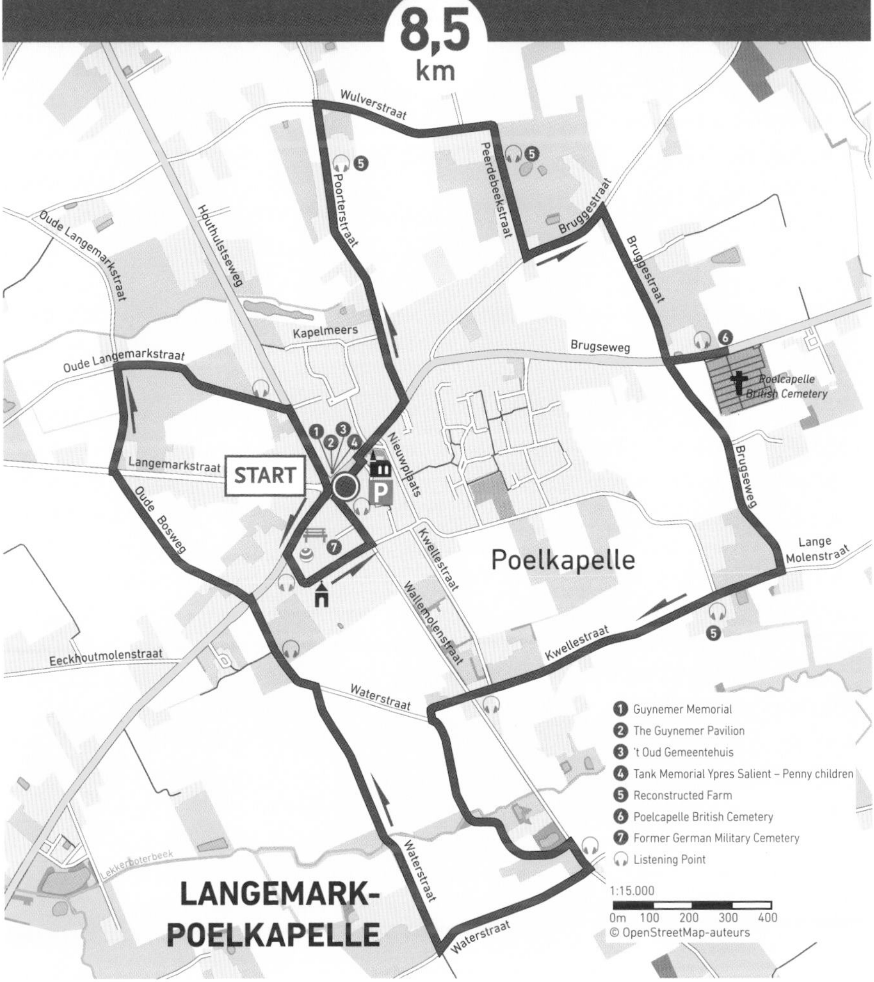

Diksmuide
Alveringem
Lo-
Reninge
Houthulst
Staden
Langemark-
Poelkapelle
Vleteren
Poperinge
Ieper
Zonnebeke

HOUTHULST

From devastated wasteland to proud and independent municipality

Because Houthulst was right on the frontline, trench warfare and its non-stop bombardments transformed the landscape into a desolate wasteland.

The municipality's modest finances were woefully inadequate to fund the necessary reconstruction. Klerken-Houthulst therefore decided to have itself 'adopted' by the Belgian State, which agreed to provide the necessary resources.

A view of Houthulst Forest
Houthulst Forest

Architect Jos Viérin was appointed to draw up the general plan for the reconstruction. Because Houthulst had been so completely destroyed, Viérin effectively started with a blank sheet of paper. This allowed him scope to give the village a major 'facelift'.

The heart of Houthulst

Viérin's masterpiece in Houthulst is the parish church. Its style reflects the modernism that was starting to become popular. Dedicated to St. John the Baptist, the church was rebuilt slightly to the north of its original site, so that it was now right at the centre of the new village. The remains of the old cemetery in the Zevende Artilleriestraat

The reconstruction of the St. John the Baptist Church
Westhoek verbeeldt

The De Groote family in 1914. Eugéne De Groote is on the left.
Westhoek verbeeldt

show where the old church once stood. All the important roads in and out of the village start at the new church, which is the symbolic heart of Houthulst.

The influence of Mayor Eugène De Groote

After the Armistice, the pre-war mayor, Eugène De Groote, was appointed as the High Royal Commissioner for the region by the Department for the Devastated Regions. In 1918, Houthulst was just a village within the larger municipality of Klerken-Houthulst. However, De Groote used his political influence to ensure that Houthulst now became an independent municipality in its own right, splitting away from Klerken in 1928. De Groote became the new municipality's first mayor.

The rebuilt St. John the Baptist Church.
(City of Kortrijk/ Image Bank)

Labourers collecting unexploded shells in Houthulst Forest.
Westhoek verbeeldt

Still clearing munitions, anno 2020

Immediately after the war, huge amounts of munitions needed to be cleared from the old battlefields. This work was mainly carried out by prisoners-of-war and Chinese labourers, although when the price of metal started to rise local people also joined in.

One-fifth of all shells did not explode
During the First World War, some 1.5 billion shells were fired. Of these, roughly one-fifth failed to explode. Even today, some 200-300 tons of munitions are recovered and made safe each year!

TIP

Theatre walk

Take part in this historic walk that will lead you past the Virgin Mary grotto, old farmhouses, the convent, the church and the 'den Trimard' tavern. Along the way, actors will perform scenes that explain the role of religion during the reconstruction.

16 and 17 May 2020

Belgian military cemetery

This cemetery is the final resting place for 1,804 soldiers, including 1,723 Belgians and 81 Italians. Most of these soldiers were killed during the Final Offensive in 1918 on 28 or 29 September. It is the second largest Belgian military cemetery. The location on the edge of the Vrijbos and the striking star (of David) plan give this place a serene, dignified character. Since 2016 a crypt on the grounds of the cemetery contains remains of unidentified war victims.

Poelkapellestraat (no. 42 and 44)
Houthulst

Feniks cycle route

Cycling past remarkable sites with remarkable stories, you will learn more about the history of DOVO (bomb disposal), the Boskasteel (Woods Castle), Château Melane and the Peace Mill.

www.feniks2020.be

Tourism
Markt 17, Houthulst
T. +32 51 46 08 97
toerisme@houthulst.be

Hours of opening:
Monday 8.30-12.00 and 14.00-16.00
Tuesday 8.30-12.00 and 14.00-16.00
Wednesday: 8.30-12.00 and 14.00-16.00
Thursday: 8.30-12.00 and 14.00-19.30
Friday: 8.30-12.00
Saturday: Closed
Sunday: Closed

The Peace Mill

This stone windmill from 1879 bears silent witness to the First World War in the Westhoek. The German army used the mill as an observation post. During the final offensive of 1918 the mill was reduced to ruins. After complete restoration, the Peace Mill was transformed into a viewing platform with a unique panorama of the historic battle-fields and the hilly landscape.

Molenweg (opposite to Nr 10), Klerken
Free entrance

KOEKELARE
Middelkerke
Nieuwpoort
Koekelare
Diksmuide
Kortemark
Houthulst
Hooglede
Staden

Koekelare and the link with France

Even before the First World War, hundreds of men and women left Koekelare each year to go and work in Northern France, mainly as seasonal workers in the beet and flax fields. In addition, many small Flemish farmers began to move in the same direction, looking to take over abandoned farms in the less densely populated French countryside. The additional losses of French farmers on the battlefields after 1914 only intensified the situation. Many Belgian refugees were also put to work in the agricultural sector, which lowered the threshold for later starting their own farms. For this reason, many of the refugees did not return home after 1918.

Born survivors. The flight and return of refugees after the First World War

The exhibition 'Born survivors. The flight and return of refugees after the First World War' illustrates the heart-breaking choices often faced by people who fled to France for safety during the war years. In particular, should they stay in France or should they go home once the fighting stopped? The answer often depended on their family situation and the availability of work. Some were so shocked by the devastation they saw when they arrived back in the Westhoek that they decided to return to France for good. Others were put off by the amount of administration the returners had to deal with before they could receive compensation, particularly in an age when most manual labourers found reading and writing far from easy. There were also families who had rented land before the war but were no longer certain whether their lease would be extended. Why come back when house prices in France were so cheap and farms were more or less there for the taking? In this way, some of the Belgian enclaves in France, particularly Normandy, continued to grow, even after the war.

After the war, clearing and levelling of agricultural land and cleaning out watercourses was hard work, carried out by hand with shovel and spade.

Born survivors. The recovery of the old front region is the story of people who were able to fend for themselves in difficult circumstances after the war.
Bruges City Archives: Brusselle-Traen Collection.

TIP

Exhibition: 'Born survivors. The flight and return of refugees after the First World War'

During the First World War, hundreds of thousands of Belgians fled their country. Most of those living near the frontline areas ended up in France. No-one imagined it would take four years before they could think about returning. The complete destruction of their homes and villages confronted many of them with a heart-rending choice. Should we go back or not? And if we go back, what will we live on? 'Born survivors' answers these questions and shows how people picked up the threads of their lives after the Armistice.

From 4 April 2020
Fransmansmuseum
('Frenchies' Museum)
Sint-Maartensplein 15b, Koekelare
T. +32 51 61 04 94
cultuurentoerisme@koekelare.be
Mon.-Thu.-Fri.: 09.30-12.00
and 13.30-17.00
Wed.-Sat.*-Sun.*-public holidays*:
13.30-17.00 (from 15/05 to 15/11)

Lange Max Museum

Here you can see the gun platform of the famous German cannon, 'Lange Max' (Long Max). After the war, the gun became a major tourist attraction, visited by (amongst others) King Albert I, the Japanese crown prince Hirohito and the British Minister of War, Winston Churchill.

Clevenstraat 2, Koekelare
T. +32 476 21 68 59
www.langemaxmuseum.be

Käthe Kollwitz Museum

This museum is devoted to the pacifist art of the German Käthe Kollwitz, who lost her son in 1914.

Sint-Maartensplein 15b, Koekelare
T. +32 51 61 04 94
www.toerismekoekelare.be

Fransmansmuseum

The Fransmansmuseum tells the story of the 'Frenchies', the seasonal workers who until the 1960s travelled to France each year to earn their living.

Sint-Maartensplein 15b, Koekelare

Koekelare Woods, with Arboretum

Koekelare has its own species of tree: the Koekelare pine. The tree is a cultivar of the Corsican pine and was first sown in 1882. After the war, more than 40 hectares were planted up with coniferous trees, including the Koekelare pine, of which fine examples can be seen in the arboretum.

Bovekerkestraat 9, Koekelare

VEURNE

Koksijde
Nieuwpoort
De Panne
Veurne
Diksmuide
Alveringem
Lo-Reninge
Houthulst

Veurne, the 'open' city

During the First World War, Veurne (Furnes) was declared to be an open city. From April 1915 onwards, under the terms of international agreements, this meant that no troops or military material could pass through it, as a result of which the 'defenceless' city would not be subject to bombardment. Even so, Veurne was regularly shelled by the Germans, so that by the end of the war some 300 buildings were seriously damaged or destroyed.

Market Square, 1918. Mission Dhuicque.
KIK-IRPA

Hôtel de l'Espérance (now 't Kasteeltje) in Nieuwpoort in the early 1920s.
Walter Lelièvre Collection

Yellow bricks from Flemish clay

Yellow bricks are typical for this north-western area of the Westhoek. Depending on the type of clay used, the bricks could either be pure yellow or have an orange or red tint. During the reconstruction, the number of brickworks increased, many of them under the name of Briqueterie de l'Yser. After a brief boom period, the Briqueterie went out of business in 1924.

The Veurne architect Camille Van Elslande helped to

Tabernacle windows on the Market Square in Veurne.
Visit Veurne

Camille Van Elslande
Ivan Winnock Collection

determine the historical character of many reconstructed buildings, often combined with modern business functions. His most important designs include the row of houses on the Market Square (nos. 31-34), the National Bank building, the row of houses in the Ooststraat (nos. 13-23) and the sugar factory.

The tabernacle window

Typical for the reconstruction in Veurne was the use of decorative tabernacle windows with a shell motif above the windows at the top of the stepped gable.

Hotel Die Nobele Rose

The 16th century building in which Hotel Die Nobele Rose was located received a direct hit from a German shell in 1914. A short while before, it had accommodated both the general staff of King Albert and Marie Curie. After the war, the building was restored by Eugène Dhuicque to his own design.

The 'Bomb' in the tower of the St. Nicholas Church

As in so many other parts of the Westhoek, the city authorities allowed Veurne to be reconstructed in a typical regional style with no major changes to layout or appearance. Even the ruined house that obscured the view of the 13-14th century tower of St. Nicholas's Church was rebuilt, much to the annoyance of some. One of the bells in the tower, dating from 1379, was known as the 'Bomb'. If you heard the 'Bomb' during the First World War, you knew there was danger!

'Bomtje' (The Bomb)

The tower of St. Nicholas Church contains the town's carillion of 47 bells, including the bell known as 'Bomtje' (Bomb), dating from 1379. If you heard the 'Bomb' during the First World War, you knew there was danger!

Hotel Die Noble Rose during the First World War.
Westhoek Verbeeldt

The tower of St. Nicholas's Church.

TIP

Feniks exhibition: The tower of St. Nicholas's Church

214 steps, a carillon with 47 bells, 11 viewing windows and a magnificent view: what more could you want! On your way to the top, you will learn about the importance of belfry towers during both world wars.

St. Nicholas Church
Appelmarkt – Veurne
T. +32 58 33 55 31
infotoerisme@veurne.be
Church tower open from 30 May 2020
Hours of opening: www.visit-veurne.be

'Free Fatherland, life behind the front' Visitors Centre

A fascinating exhibition about the last small area of unoccupied Belgium during the First World War.

Grote Markt 29, Veurne
www.vrijvaderland.be

Kasteel Beauvoorde

Kasteel Beauvoorde is considered the best-kept secret of the Westhoek. An eccentric nobleman bought the residence in the 19th century and had it restored to 17th-century tastes. A stately home with a story that will captivate knights both young and old.

Wulveringmstraat 10, Veurne
T. +32 58 29 92 29

Bakery Museum

In the Bakery Museum you walk around in a bakery where time stands still and you can bake your own bread, in groups if you like.

Albert I-laan 2, Veurne
T. +32 58 31 38 97

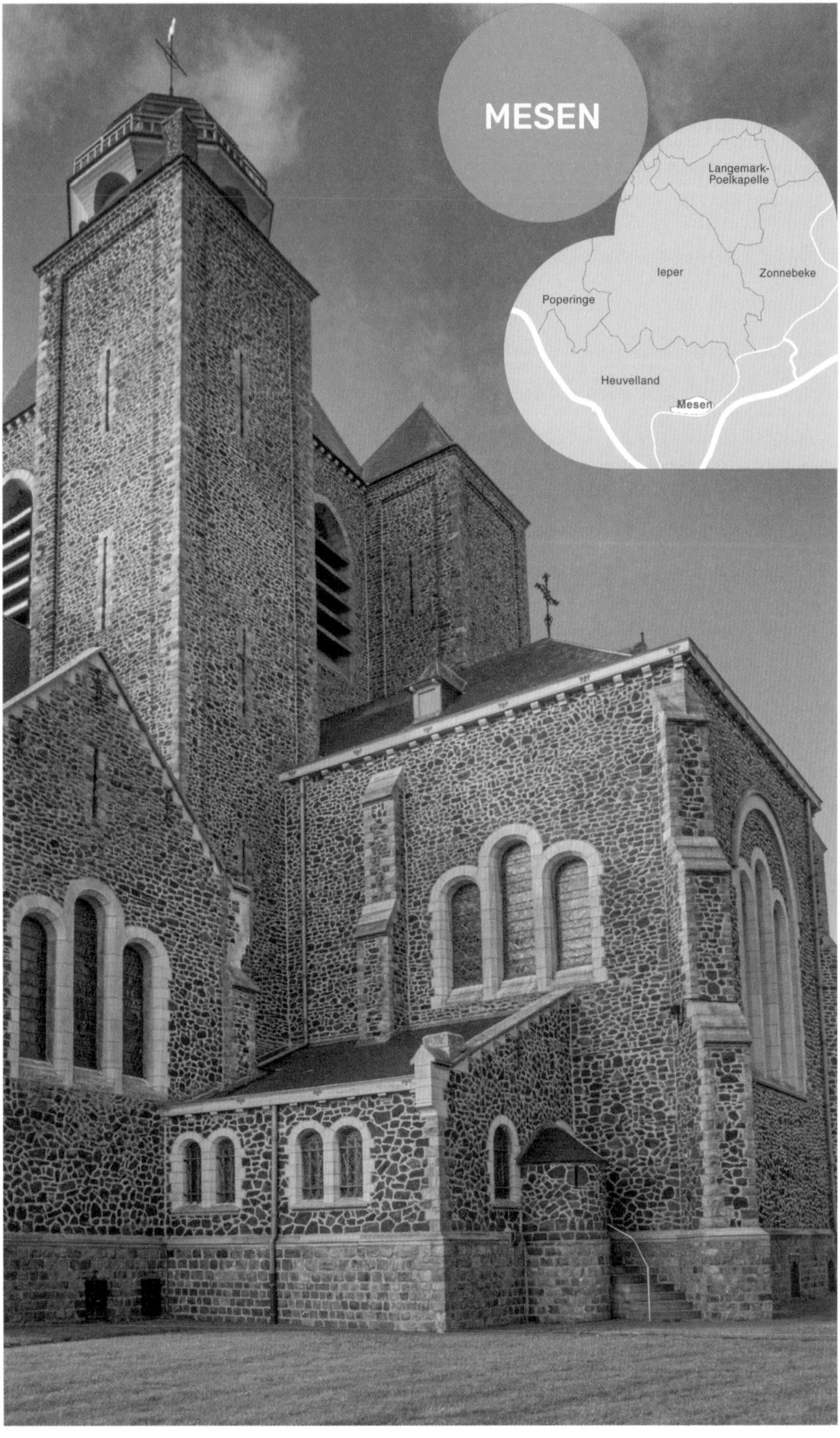
MESEN
Langemark-
Poelkapelle
Ieper
Zonnebeke
Poperinge
Heuvelland
Mesen

A small town with a great history

Because of its strategic location, the small and sleepy provincial town of Mesen (Messines) found itself in the middle of the fighting during the First World War, with the Mine Battle of 1917 as its climax. The town was completely destroyed.

All that was left of the Daalstraat and the Royal Foundation building, 1919.
Mesen Historical Museum Collection

> **Camille Castelle**
> *'My brother came to have a look in '18, when he was a soldier. Everything was flattened. My father also came to have a look at Mesen. In '20, when we returned, the church was just a pile of rubble. Grass was growing out of it. You couldn't see it had ever been a church.*

From 1919 onwards, about 1,000 of the town's original 1,500 inhabitants returned. Often left to fend for themselves, they lived in self-made shelters or in small barrack villages, like Dekenie.

The first house in Mesen on the corner of the Ieperstraat and the Nieuwkerkestraat. *Johan Beun Collection)*

> **Lucien Loridan**
> *"My second brother came with the news. There was a way to get a grant of 3,000 francs to buy materials. So me and my eldest brother went back to Mesen together. We began to clear things up straight away. We found lodging in the home of the local café owner, the best that was available. Before long, we started building a barrack."*

During the reconstruction, a number of major changes were made on the market square. The new town hall was built in the centre, where the old vicarage and the municipal boy's school once stood. The boy's school was moved to the site of the old girl's schools, with the girl's moving to a new site on the former town cemetery.

Virginie, the munitions train

During the early years of the war, the Germans built a narrow-gauge railway through the town. Because all the roads had been destroyed, this Decauville railway was used after the Armistice to bring in new materials and to take away rubble from the ruins. The steam train regularly blew its whistle, so that it became a kind of travelling clock. It was known by local people as 'Virginie'.

The Market Square at the start of the 1930s. On the left, there is an open space where the town hall (now the Tourist Info-point) will be built in 1933-1934.
Mesen Historical Museum Collection

The market square, with the Decauville railway.

The Royal Foundation and some of its pupils, seen from the Waastenstraat in 1919.
Johan Beun

The Royal Foundation in Mesen

From 1776 onwards, the Royal Foundation in Mesen cared for the education and maintenance of the children of soldiers who died or became invalids as a result of their service to the state. After the First World War, the Foundation moved to Lede, near Aalst. This was a serious loss for the town.

The church today.
Westtoer

A peace carillon as a symbol of reconciliation

The peace carillon in the St. Nicholas Church consists of 58 bells, donated by various local and international organisations as a symbol of reconciliation. Every 30 minutes the carillon plays well-known music from the countries involved in the First World War.

A surprise under the main choir

During clearance work in 1923, a previously unknown medieval crypt was discovered. This has been restored and can now be visited.

TIP

St. Nicholas Church. Exhibition: 'A small town with a great history'

Half way up the 214 steps of the church tower, this exhibition highlight different facets of life in Mesen over the centuries. Climb right to the top and you can enjoy a fantastic view with a pair of panoramic binoculars. On the way, you will pass the bells of the peace carillon.

St. Nicholas Church
Featherstonplein, Mesen
T. +32 57 22 17 14
info@mesen.be
www.mesen.be
The church tower will open in the late summer of 2020, daily from 09.00 to 17.00

Tourist Info-point (TIP)

The TIP is the natural starting point for every visit to our peace town.

Markt 1, Mesen

St. Nicholas Church

This former abbey church dates originally from 1057, but was completely rebuilt (1928) following its destruction in the First World War. The church tower offers a splendid view over the surrounding countryside. Nearby, there is a memorial plaque to the memory of a soldier from New Zealand, Samuel Frickleton, VC.

Featherstonplein, Mesen

Irish Peace Park – a national symbol for Ireland in the Westhoek

Young people from both Northern Ireland and Southern Ireland built this tower, as a symbol of peace and reconciliation.

Armentierssteenweg, Mesen

LO-RENINGE

Veurne
Diksmuide
Alveringem
Lo-
Reninge
Houthulst
Vleteren
Ieper

The Feniks in Lo-Reninge

Because of their different positions in the front zone, the four villages of Lo-Reninge each have a different reconstruction history. Noordschote was razed to the ground. In Reninge just 54 buildings were left standing. In Lo, a quarter of the houses were in ruins. Pollinkhove was relatively spared.

The reconstruction of public property in Noordschote, Reninge and Lo was supported by the Department for the Devastated Regions. The rebuilding work in Noordschote was left in the hands of the High Royal Commissioner. In Reninge, Mayor Amandus Sticker had the final responsibility for the reconstruction.

Architects were appointed by the government. Charles Laloo drew the plans for Noordschote. Charles Pil and Henri Carbon did the same for Reninge. In Lo, the innovative ideas of Henri Lacoste to modernise the town met with resistance. His plans were amended, so that there were only a few minor changes to the main streets.

Repair of the landscape and reconstruction of the agricultural infrastructure was

'Yellow bricks'

Two brick factories were set up by the 'Briqueteries del' Yser' company at Pollinkhove (1919) and Reninge (1922). They provided the municipal warehouses in Lo and Reninge with their typical yellow bricks.

Reconstruction of the market square in Lo.
Jozef Camerlynck collection

supported by the State Service for Agricultural Recovery, the Boerenbond (Farmers' Union) and local farming associations. Local savings societies and lending clubs played an important role by providing loans that made it possible for both citizens and farmers to start their rebuilding work with a minimum of delay. As a result, agricultural production in Lo-Reninge was resumed reasonably quickly.

The St. Rictrudis Church in Reninge, rebuilt in 1923.
Chris Vandewalle Collection

Lacoste

In Lo, the planning of the reconstruction went less smoothly. The innovative ideas of architect Henri Lacoste (1885-1968) met with considerable local resistance. He wanted to modernise the town by prioritising public hygiene, sanitation and healthy living conditions, but with due respect for its historic monuments. His plans envisaged a pedestrian boulevard, a commercial district and new approach roads, all set in 'green' surroundings. However, his proposals were rejected in favour of a traditional reconstruction, with only minor amendments to some of the main streets.

Father Tommelein

Father Aloïs Tommelein (1857-1944) walked 20 kilometres every day from his temporary accommodation at the Abbey of St. Sixtus in West-Vleteren to tend to the religious needs of the returnees in Noordschote. His main concern was not the rebuilding of his church or his vicarage, but the building of emergency housing for his parishioners. He lived like a missionary and worked alongside the people with his bare hands.

Cycling route

A cycling route of 36 kilometres leads you to all the most important reconstruction sites in Lo-Reninge, with information boards at 28 key locations. The route brochure is available at the local tourist office.

Tourist Office: Lauka
Markt 17, Lo-Reninge
T. +32 58 28 91 66
info@lauka.be

TIP

Destrooper Visitors' centre

Here you discover the rich history of the biscuits of the Biscuiterie Jules Destrooper. Part of the Visitor's Centre is also dedicated to the First World War. The son of the founder Jules Destrooper, Jules Destrooper Junior, was dismissed from military service for illness and returned to his home Lo. The biscuit factory was closed due to temporary shortages and he decided to publish postcards. These postcards contain views from the region and typical war scenes. The front soldiers eagerly grabbed these cards to send home. The collection contained around 150 different cards. Today you can see part of the collection at the Destrooper Visitors' Centre.

Gravestraat 5, Lo
T. +32 58 28 09 33

CWGC

From Recovery to Remembrance: The Commonwealth War Graves Commission in Flanders after the First World War

During the First World War men and women from across the world served with forces of the British Empire on land, at sea and in the air. It was clear the death toll would be unprecedented.

In 1917, the Imperial (now Commonwealth) War Graves Commission was established to create formal cemeteries and memorials commemorating those who died. A partnership between the UK, Australia, Canada & Newfoundland, India, New Zealand and South Africa, the Commissions duty was to ensure the dead would be honoured equally – regardless of rank or background.

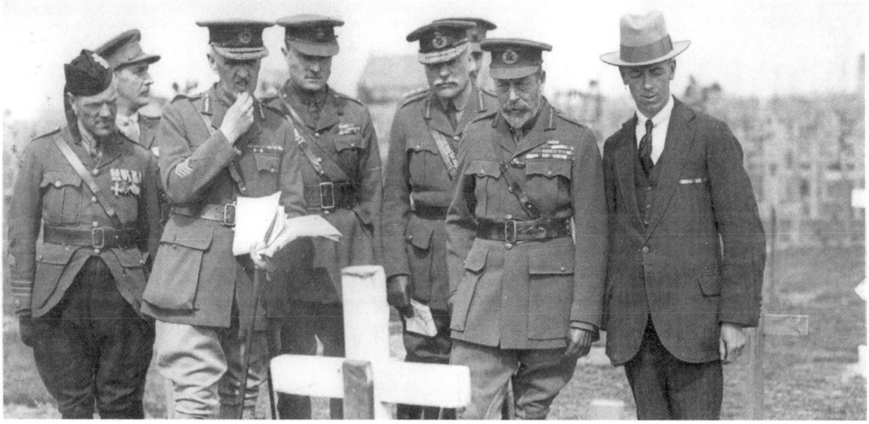

King George V, accompanied by Fabian Ware and Earl Haig, inspects the wooden crosses at Tyne Cot Cemetery during his pilgrimage to the battlefields, 11 May 1922.
CWGC

The Commonwealth War Graves Commission cares worldwide for the graves and memorials of 1.7 million men and women of the Commonwealth who died during the two World Wars.

The Commission works across 23,000 locations in more than 150 countries and territories throughout the world, and is committed to maintaining these sites for evermore.

The work of the Commonwealth War Graves Commission continues

Today a team of 1,300 staff care for cemeteries and memorials on every continent except Antarctica. From gardeners and stonemasons to historians and archivists, the 'global family' preserves the CWGC's rich heritage. The CWGC still recovers and reburies more than 30 casualties each year in Belgium and France, ensuring they receive a dignified burial.

In 2019 we opened our first visitor centre, The CWGC Experience, to share our work with the public.

Based on the principles:

- Each of the Commonwealth dead should be commemorated by name on a headstone or memorial
- Headstones and memorials should be uniform and permanent
- There should be equality of treatment for the war dead irrespective of rank or religion

TIP

From Recovery to Remembrance – About the exhibition

After the First World War there was much debate about how and The newly-formed Imperial War Graves Commission (IWGC) was at the centre of public anger about the war dead not being repatriated home and how they would be commemorated.

From Recovery to Remembrance explores the complexities and controversies of key decisions the IWGC made as it undertook the mammoth task of commemorating 1.1 million casualties, 194,000 from Belgium. With competing creative visions and the pressure to rebuild quickly after the war, we reveal the behind-the-scenes story of how the Commission began to shape the landscapes of remembrance we know today. Alongside a wealth of archive images and never-before-seen documents are displayed artefacts recovered from the former battlefields, giving a powerful insight into the strenuous efforts to bury the dead with dignity.

CWGC Ypres Information Centre
Menenstraat 33, Ypres

1 April to 15 November 2020
Tuesday to Sunday: 13.00-21.00.
Friday and Saturday: 10.00–21.00
T. +32 57 35 27 91
enquiries@cwgc.org
www.cwgc.org

“ Winston Churchill, Secretary of State for War, 1919

'A more sacred place for the British race does not exist in the world.'

Cycle routes 14-18

Explore the Westhoek via the 14-18 cycle routes. These circular routes connect the various monuments, cemeteries and museums that commemorate the war. They are an excellent way to discover the old wartime landscape. You can order the route brochures via shop.westtoer.be or purchase them from local tourist offices in the Westhoek.

Tourist car routes 14-18

Discover the wartime landscape of the Westhoek by car or motorbike using these six new vehicle routes, which are collected together on a handy summary map. The map and the individual route brochures can be ordered via shop.westtoer.be or purchased from local tourist offices in the Westhoek. Alternatively, you can use your smartphone or tablet to access the app 'Autoroutes Eerste Wereldoorlog in de Westhoek' (Tourist routes 14-18: by car). This app contains photos, texts, documents and sound fragments.

www.flandersfields.be

colophon

'From the Ashes' was produced by Westtoer apb, in collaboration with local towns, municipalities and associations in the Westhoek and with the support of Toerisme Vlaanderen (Visit Flanders).

TEXTS
Simon Augustyn (Stad Diksmuide), Dries Claeys (In Flanders Fields Museum, Ieper), Dominiek Dendooven (In Flanders Fields Museum, Ieper), Karen Derycke (Memorial Museum Passchendaele 1917, Zonnebeke), Hannelore Franck (Yper Museum, Ieper), Chris Vandewalle (Stad Diksmuide), Annemie Morisse (Stad Poperinge) en Commonwealth War Graves Commission

TRANSLATION
Ian Connerty

EDITING
karakters.be

MAPS
Peggy Andries, Westtoer

LAYOUT
karakters.be

PHOTOGRAPHY
Westtoer, Jan Dhondt

PRINTING
Lowyck drukkerij

CONCEPT AND COORDINATION
Stephen Lodewyck (Westtoer)

IMAGE CREDITS
cf. captions, Collectie Jozef Camerlynck, Westtoer

RESPONSIBLE PUBLISHER
Westtoer apb
Koning Albert I-laan 120,
8200 Sint-Michiels (Brugge)

D/3029/2019/62
ISBN 978-9-49234-655-1